To: Mary
a very special
friend

Love ya

Ruthie
Hernandez

A Father's Love

by

Ruthie M. Hernandez

authorHOUSE

1663 LIBERTY DRIVE, SUITE 200
BLOOMINGTON, INDIANA 47403
(800) 839-8640
www.authorhouse.com

First published by AuthorHouse 07/28/04

ISBN: 1-4184-7516-5 (sc)
ISBN: 1-4184-7517-3 (dj)

Library of Congress Control Number: 2004095147

Printed in the United States of America
Bloomington, Indiana

This book is printed on acid-free paper.

This book is dedicated to my loving and beautiful sister Lisa Sendejas.

I want to thank you for all of the love and compassion you gave to me throughout my childhood and even now through my adulthood. I have never felt alone, knowing that I have you as my sister. I love you, Sis and I will never forget all the love and sacrifices you gave to me and all of our brothers and sisters. I know you have made our father very proud!!!

1

It was a Saturday afternoon and our family was getting ready to go to the beach. We lived about eight blocks from the beach, on an island in southeast Texas. It was so nice there; everywhere you look, we were surrounded by water. I loved going to the beach on the weekends. My dad would cut the biggest watermelon we'd ever seen and it was always so sweet. We would play and swim for hours and it was always so much fun playing with all my brothers and sisters.

My father never seemed stressed about having so many kids. My mom was the same way; she would clean the whole house and cook every day for all of us. My mom always did everything around the house. Our house was always so clean and neat. I was always so proud of my parents.

When a holiday came, my parents would buy us two outfits for all special occasions, one for church and one for play. I always looked forward to holidays with my family. I remember my mom telling us, people always complimented her on how well-kept we all were. I loved my family. The only thing I wished for was that Daddy didn't have to work so much. But there were so many of us to feed and take care of, so I kind of understood why Daddy worked a lot.

I had five brothers and three sisters, and my parents were having another baby in October. So, as you can see, that is a big family and we are still growing. Today was a great day for all of us. We loved going to the beach with Mom and Dad. It was always so wonderful being a part of such a great family. My mom told us today we were going to have one of my dad's cousins come and stay with us. We had never met this cousin. We knew most of our parents' family, but this cousin was a second cousin to my daddy.

Our cousin was going to work for my dad or my uncles and save his money to help support his family in Mexico. My mom told us they are poor and our cousin is the son of my grandmother's sister. She said he was a few years older than my oldest brother. We really didn't think too much about it. I guessed he would be sharing a room with the boys, since he was a boy too. When we saw our parents getting ready for him to come and stay with us, I asked my mom, "How long will he be staying with us?"

Mom looked at me and said, "For as long as he needs to." We were okay with that since my parents were okay with it.

All of the younger kids were in Catholic school. My parents were very involved with the church and the school. I remember on Sundays, my mom would take us to church and my father would be in the church cafeteria helping make tamales to raise money for the school and the church. I was in the sixth grade then, and I loved school and my life. We went to church six times a week, every day except Saturday. Since it was a Catholic school, church was part of our schooling. My mom was always a room mother and she would bring punch and cupcakes or cookies to our classrooms for class parties during all special holidays. I always seemed to love when my mom helped out at school. I felt that even with so many kids, she still took time to donate for the school, church, and us. All my friends would tell me how nice my mom was and that they always liked her cupcakes. That always made me feel good when I heard these compliments about my own mother.

Holidays were always special in our home. We always went to church, and afterwards, our family had a barbeque for the celebration part of the holiday. I always enjoyed Easter Sundays. All of our cousins and their parents went to a huge park near our homes. We always had a massive Easter egg hunt. Gosh, after church, we couldn't wait to hurry home and change into our play outfits that Mom had already bought for us to wear to the park. We had so much fun the whole entire day. All the teenagers played volleyball and other different types of games, while all the adults seemed to have a lot of fun too, just being together as a family.

I remember one year, my mom came to my school with my older brother for our Halloween party. He was dressed as King Kong. Mom was holding him by this huge chain. It went around his neck and Mom looked like she was holding it pretty tight. He looked so real. He scared all the smaller kids, and the older ones thought he looked pretty cool.

I remember when they came to my class. I was in the fifth grade at the time, and he would walk from side to side just like a real ape; everyone was laughing. He then scratched under his arm and smelled his finger. Then he would scratch again and sniff his finger. He kept on and on, just keeping the kids laughing. I could tell my mom was getting mad at him for being bad, but he just kept on as long as the kids would keep laughing.

I loved my brother; he was such a great brother. This is just one example of what my brothers would do for any of us. Here is an introduction to my immediate family and a little bit about each one of them. First of all, my oldest brother is Louis; he was married and he had a daughter. My niece's name is Cassie. She was the prettiest baby I had ever seen. I loved them so much.

I remember one day when I was younger. Louis came over to our house and he had bought me a couple of coloring books and some crayons. I had the mumps during that time. So I wasn't feeling too great. When he arrived at our home, he asked me if I felt any better. I told him yes because I actually did feel better from his warm gesture. I remember he smiled at me and I felt so loved by my brother that day. I always thought that was so cool of him to do, even though he

3

had his own little family to take care of. From that day on, I knew I had a special brother.

My second oldest brother is William—we called him Willie. He was also married and was in the army. I really missed Willie when he would leave. I always thought Willie was so smart and so handsome. I remember he sent us a picture of himself jumping out of a plane. You see, Willie was a paratrooper in the U.S. Army. I remember I felt so afraid to see him like that. But Daddy said, "Willie is tough, you don't need to worry about Willie, he is as smart as a whip."

I thought to myself that if Daddy says he is all right then Willie will be all right. So I tried not to worry about him anymore after that.

Willie also had a baby who was my first nephew. He was such a good baby; I loved holding him. My nephew's name is William Jr. We called him Wick for short. He always smiled and kicked his feet when we played with him. My sister-in-law let me hold Wick for as long as I wanted to. I used to hold Wick till my arm ached. But I didn't care, I just loved holding him. And I know he loved me holding him too. I loved being an aunt to these two great babies. It kind of made me feel grown knowing that I was an aunt.

Then there was my third brother, Hector, who was in the army also. He was stationed in Alaska. He would always write all of us and put a big sun in the top corner of the page. We loved reading his letters. He had never been in the snow before, so it was very hard for him to be away from our home, where it never really snowed.

Hector was cool. When he came home on leave, Hector always took the time to play with all of us. Hector had showed me how to fight so that I could protect myself. Then there were days when Hector would play army with all of the little ones. We would march up and down the stairs in our house and all through the rooms. It was so much fun. But I hated when he had to leave. I felt so sorry for Hector; sometimes I felt like he didn't want to leave either. Daddy kept telling us that Hector would be back before we know it.

After Hector, I have an older sister, Lisa. She was so pretty, all my friends used to tell me how pretty she is. My mom and dad had four boys before they had Lisa. I think that my mom and dad had to have been pretty excited when they had Lisa, since all their children were only boys.

I loved my sister so much. She was a nice, cool sister, not mean and grouchy like some sisters my friends had. That made life so great. I used to like to watch Lisa get ready in the mornings. She always put her makeup on so nicely. I was so proud to say that was my sister.

My parents had a baby; their oldest son died when he was a few months old from pneumonia. At that time, my father was a gunnery sergeant in the U.S. Army. His name was Luis, just like Dad's. So when he died, Mom and Dad named my second brother Louis, still close to Daddy's name but a little different. I had seen pictures from my brother's funeral and my parents looked so sad.

Luis was so pretty, he almost looked like a little girl. Daddy was dressed in his army uniform for the funeral. I guess that's why a few of my family members followed in his footsteps and joined the army also. After Lisa, my parents had my sister Priscilla; we called her Lilly. Lilly was two years older than me and she was cool. She really never fought with me or any of us.

I did know one thing that would make Lilly mad and that would be not putting Daddy first. Lilly was very protective of Daddy. She would tell anyone off, even the neighbors if they said anything negative about our family or Daddy. One day I remember our next door neighbors were teasing us about Daddy never being home and that we only had a mom. Lilly wanted to fight them. From that day on, I knew she would always stick up for me or us if we needed her to.

My parents had me after Lilly. I am named after my mom; my name is Ruthie. I asked my mom one day why she named me after herself and not Lisa, and she said because I looked just like her. I kind of liked that idea because everyone used to tell me how pretty my mom is. I used to think to myself that when Daddy was extra nice to me, maybe it was because I reminded him of Mom. Either way, I thought my parents were both great and good-looking.

My brother after me is Michael. He was kind of shy, but I loved him as my brother. He was so handsome, just like Daddy. Michael loved going places with Daddy. Michael played with all of us pretty well. I really don't remember any of us fighting or not getting along with one another. After my brother Michael, my parents had Sandra and Ralph; they were the youngest. Sandra was so cute—she looked just like Daddy too. Her middle name was Louise to match my daddy's, which is Luis. Sandra was really tiny when she was little. I always thought that she would take after my mom, who is pretty short.

After Sandra is Ralph. Ralph was the cutest out of all of us, I thought. He had long curls when he was a baby and he was a little husky, which made him even cuter. Everyone always told Mom and Dad how cute Ralphy was. Ralph is named after my father's boss. His boss' name is. Ralph Tomas. Daddy was always so proud of Ralph. But he was really very fond of Mr. Ralph and he respected his boss. I always thought that was so cool of my father to name his son after his boss.

I remember Daddy would take the younger boys over to see Mr. Ralph and his family quite a bit. Michael and Ralph always said they had a great time there. This year, Ralph was getting ready to start kindergarten in August. He was going to have the same kindergarten teacher all of us had. Her name was Mrs. Sunseri, and we all loved her. I still remember when I walked in with my mom and daddy for my first day of kindergarten; I saw my name on a big, clear book bag with a big flap in the front. It closed with two big buttons. I looked up at daddy and asked him, "Why does my name look funny on the book bag?"

He laughed and said "Oh, they spelled your name as Ruth not Ruthie, that's why it looks so funny to you."

I then looked at the book bag and said, "But why does it say that, Daddy, when you call me Ruthie, not Ruth?"

Then before I could get upset, Daddy walked over to Mrs. Sunseri and said, "Can you please change Ruthie's book bag to spell her name as Ruthie? You see, we call her Ruthie at home, and I think she will feel so much better if her bag was to say Ruthie."

Mrs. Sunseri looked at me and smiled, and then she said, "Oh Ruthie, I'm so sorry. I will change it right now for you, okay?" Then Mrs. Sunseri changed the name on my bag right then and there. That day, I knew she would be the nicest teacher ever. I knew I was going to love being in her class. I knew she would be just as nice to my little brother Ralph, now that he was in her kindergarten class.

Since our school was a private Catholic school, we wore uniforms. The girls wore maroon skirts with white blouses. The blouse had a tie on it that matched our skirt, and the back of the shirt had a sailor flap on it. It was cool; I really loved our uniforms. The boys wore blue pants with a maroon shirt that matched our skirts, or they wore an all-white shirt with blue pants. I always thought they looked handsome in their uniforms. Sometimes I wore shorts under my skirt because I didn't want to show my underpants when I played outside at recess. I really enjoyed being at such a great school.

2

Well, today was the day that my cousin was to come from Mexico. I saw Mom getting the rooms and the house ready for his arrival. We were playing in front of the house when I saw Dad's car pull into the driveway. I looked inside the car and I saw this man who kind of looked like my dad's family. He had a lot of my dad's family's features. Mom and Dad introduced him to us and he seemed nice. He was kind of quiet, although he didn't speak any English. I guess he was probably nervous, being so far away from his family and not really knowing any of us or Daddy's family. I saw my mom and my dad speak to him, but most of the kids didn't speak any Spanish. My older brother spoke Spanish and he would talk to him quite a bit. They seemed to get along okay, I guess because they were pretty close to the same age.

His being there really didn't bother any of us. But as time went on, I wondered why my sister Lilly just did not seem to like him. I saw her stick her tongue at him and then run up the stairs and laugh. One time, I remember my mom saw her and ran after her and spanked her for it. When Mom spanked her, I could tell Lilly got real

9

mad. Mom told her that she better not ever do that again. Lilly didn't seem to care about Mom being angry or that she just got spanked.

I asked Lilly that night, why did she stick her tongue out at Arturo? Lilly laughed and said she did not like him because Mom treated him so nice. I really didn't think too much about it after that. I just knew Lilly meant it when she said she didn't like him.

My mom was starting to get bigger from the baby. I think it was getting close to the time for Mom to have the baby. Then Mom told me one day "Ruthie, I want you to be nice to your cousin, okay? He is very far from home." Mom also said that Arturo was a very nice man and he likes all of us. I didn't see any reason why I should not be nice to Arturo. After all, he was Daddy's cousin and he was always doing things around the house for Mom. I told Mom I would be nice to him. I was always very pleasant to him after that, but he was always nice to me. Mom just smiled at me and said that we don't want his family to worry about him or anything like that. I agreed; I would want my family not to worry either. Plus, if I had to stay with another family, I would hope that they would be nice to me too.

Then Mom just started talking about Arturo. She started saying that our cousin Arturo was a very handsome man and he should have a girlfriend. I really didn't comment because to me he was a grown man and my cousin. But as a little girl in the sixth grade, I thought he was okay. All I remember is that he never made me mad at him or anything like that. I guess Mom was starting to get pretty close to him, since his family was so far away. My father was at work a lot, so he really didn't spend too much time around Arturo. Gosh, we all missed him so much when he was gone. I always wished he didn't have to work so much. Dad was a president for the longshoreman's association on the waterfront, so he had a lot of responsibility. He had thousands of men under him.

Daddy would go to different states for work. He always traveled to conventions, being gone a few days or maybe two weeks. I really don't remember him being gone to a convention for over two weeks. So that was pretty cool that we didn't have to be too long without Daddy. I remember a few of the places Dad went to were New York

A Father's Love

and Florida. Daddy said he went everywhere around the United States that had water. I always thought that was pretty cool.

Different people from my father's job came to our home for advice from my father. I always thought that was really cool also. I always thought my father was a very smart man. I think everyone knew that because my father was president and ran the waterfront for 30 years. Gosh, I remember I loved when Daddy would come back from a convention out of state. We were always so happy to see him and so was Mom. My mom would take care of everything while Daddy was gone. Mom was pretty good at handling all of us without Daddy there.

My parents were getting ready for my cousin Tony's wedding and all of us were going. Tony is the son of my father's brother Antonio. We always called my Uncle Antonio "Uncle Tony" just like my cousin's name. My cousin Tony was marrying Rosie. I really liked Rosie. She was always so nice to me and my sisters. Plus I always thought she was so pretty.

The day of the wedding, we danced and ate and had a great time. I saw my mom dancing with my dad. Then, the rest of the night, I saw her dance with my cousin Arturo. He was the one who had come and stayed with us. All of my family seemed to have a great time at the wedding. I saw all of my dad's family there and even some of my mom's. They were all such good-looking people I was always so proud of all of them. All of their spouses were very attractive too.

My mom's family was pretty close with my father's family. So that made all functions so much more fun for all of the kids. My dad comes from a very large and very close family and I loved that. Everyone seemed so happy to see one another, it made me love my family even more. Soon after the wedding, my mom had a baby girl. They named her Patricia. During Mom's stay in the hospital, Arturo stayed at the hospital pretty late with her. I guess he had gotten very close with Mom, so he wanted to make sure she was all right.

One day, I walked in from school with all my younger brothers and sister, and my mom was by the clothes dryer, folding clothes. I asked her where the baby was and she said, "In my bedroom. Be real quiet and all of you can go see her." I took Ralph's hand and Michael had Sandra's hand, and we started walking towards Mom's

11

bedroom. We were trying our best to be real quiet just like Mom said. Then when we walked into the bedroom, we stood in front of the crib and just watched her sleep. It was pretty neat knowing that I had another little sister to play with all of us. Now with Mom back at home with the baby, I hoped she wouldn't be as tired anymore. Mom seemed really tired a lot while she was pregnant. Daddy was at work but I know he was probably very happy about having a new daughter. I looked over at my mom and she looked so nice and thin already. Mom always had such a great looking figure, so even right after having a baby she still looked nice. My sister looked so peaceful and pretty I could tell everyone was happy to welcome her to our family.

A few weeks later, my parents were having a going away party for my cousin Arturo. I guessed he had saved enough money for his family by now, so it was time for him to go back to Mexico. Arturo had been with us a year already. It sure didn't seem like he had been there that long. But now mom says it is time for him to go back home. Most of my aunts and uncles were there at the party, also some of my parents' friends. We had a good time; we liked every time my parents had parties, because that meant all our cousins our age were coming over. We would all play together and have a great time. Mom said we always had parties at our home because it was easier than taking so many kids to some of our aunts' and uncles' homes. Everyone always seemed to have a great time at all my parents' parties.

I remember that night of Arturo's going away party. All of the kids were playing hide and seek and I went to hide in my parents' room. While I was hiding, my sister and I saw a large suitcase. We looked at each other, and before I knew it, we were opening the suitcase. Just as we did we felt a slap on our shoulder. My mom was standing behind us, saying, "What the hell are you doing?" I looked up at her and I asked her why her clothes were in the suitcase, and she said "The clothes don't fit me anymore. I am going to send them to the Goodwill." Then before I knew it, Mom said, "I want all of you to get out of my room and go back outside and play."

We went back outside and my sister Lilly was mad at my mom for slapping us; I guess I was too. After everyone left, we were getting ready for bed, and I saw my mom in the kitchen. As I walked towards her, I asked her, "Mom, those clothes in the suitcase still fit you. I saw you wear that dress last week to church. Why are you giving them away?"

She looked at me and just said "Don't worry about it; go to your room and stay out of mine." I went to my room wondering why she was so mad and in a bad mood. I went to bed and tried hard to fall asleep. I tried not to think about the slap I received from mom today. So I told myself to just forget all about it. The next day, we went to school and I thought everything was back to normal. My mom and our cousin walked with us to school. Then my mom told me that she wanted me to start walking all the kids home from school. She started telling me that from now on, she could not walk to the school and get my little brother because it was too hard with my new baby sister.

I said okay. She started telling me how to pick him up from his class and hold his hand all the way home. I knew I could do that. My other two older sisters were in middle school and high school, so this was up to me. So I started walking Michael, Sandra and Ralph home from school every day. Two days went by, and my cousin Arturo left. He told us bye and I said bye too. I felt a little sad to see him leave. Lilly told me she was glad he was leaving. I felt kind of sad because he was nice to me. But Lilly kept telling me she hated him. She said he would get Mom to buy him cigarettes and stuff. Lilly just kept saying that she was glad he was leaving. She also said Mom would make him good meals and make Daddy a burrito.

I looked at her and I said, "Yeah, but he is real nice to Mom." But I also thought maybe he was just being grateful for all Moms' help too.

Lilly just kept saying, "I am just glad he is leaving." We got ready for bed that evening and I looked over at Lilly. She looked so happy now that our cousin had left. I just thought to myself that no one comes before Daddy, not even his cousin in Lilly's eyes!

3

A few days after our cousin left, when I was in school, I heard my name over the intercom. The secretary, Mrs. Pachini, said for me to come to the library to meet with Sister Jean, our school principal. I was wondering what Sister Jean wanted with me. As I was walking, I heard Mrs. Pacini call for my brothers and my sister too. When we all arrived at the library, Sister Jean walked in and sat down. Sister Jean looked a little sad and worried. I then asked her if there was anything wrong and she said, "I want all of you to go to your classrooms and get all your things to go home. Your uncle Max will be picking you up very shortly."

I looked up at her and said, "Is everything all right, Sister Jean?"

She just looked at me and said, "Your uncle will explain everything to you, Ruthie, when he gets here."

I then asked Sister Jean, "Are my mom and dad okay?"

Sister Jean just looked up at me and said, "You need to ask your uncle when he gets here."

I felt myself getting a little nervous. Then, as I looked out the window, I saw my uncle Max coming toward the library. Uncle Max is one of my father's brothers. I saw such a sad look on his face, I really started getting scared. Uncle Max walked in and started talking to Sister Jean. I then told my brothers and sister to go to their class and get their things. As we were all walking back to the library, I could not help feeling scared at what my uncle was going to tell us. I felt it had to be pretty serious for my uncle to pick us up in the middle of the day from school.

We all walked into the library, and my uncle walked over to us and said, "Okay kids, let's go." All of us just followed him back to his car. My uncle was holding Ralph and Sandra's hand while Michael and I followed. Inside the car was so quiet; I was so scared but I didn't want to ask any questions. I didn't want to scare the kids; they were just playing with each other, not knowing that in just a few minutes, we were about to be told news that would change all of us for the rest of our lives.

When we arrived at our home, I noticed two of my other uncles' cars and my father's as well in our driveway. We walked in and my two older sisters were there as well. I looked around and I didn't see my mother anywhere. Everyone looked so sad; I was afraid to ask what was wrong, and where our mother was. I remember I walked into the kitchen and saw my father crying. My uncles had such an empty look on their faces. I was really starting to get more scared than before. As I built up the courage to ask, I looked at my father and said, "Daddy, what's wrong, where is Mom?" He looked at me with such a sad look on his face, I was afraid to hear what his answer was.

Then he answered, "She left, she left all of us."

I looked at him and said, "What do you mean she left? When is she coming back?"

He just looked at me and said, "She's not going to come back." Daddy just looked down at a paper bag that was on the table. I looked around the room and everyone was so sad and quiet. Then I noticed that the brown paper bag on the table had writing on it. I looked at the bag and I saw it was Mom's handwriting. I saw that Mom wrote "I am leaving you," then I couldn't read anymore. Suddenly Daddy picked up the brown paper bag and walked into the other room with it. Then it hit me that Mom did leave Daddy, but she also left all of us.

How could she do this to all of us and just write it down on a brown paper bag? The same bags she used to make all of our lunches. I then started crying and sat on the stairs in our living room. All the adults were talking and talking for such a long time. My oldest sister Lisa was in the kitchen with all of them. Lisa looked real scared and confused. I started to look around me; my younger brothers and my little sister were just watching television. They didn't even know anything yet, and when they were told, I didn't know if they would be able to understand the severity of all of this. I just kept thinking to myself, *what are we going to do without a mom?*

Then I looked at my father and thought, *how he is going to be without my mom? What could be so bad to make Mom do something this horrible to her family? What could be so bad to make a mother leave all her children and her husband? Where was our mom and who was she with? How long will she be gone?*

We never were without Mom except for a couple of days when she went to the hospital to have a baby. Even then, Mom seemed to get everything ready days before her stay at the hospital. So we as kids never really took care of ourselves or the house without Mom. The family I thought was so great was now separated and lost. My mom was always here when we came home from school; how were going to function without our rock? She kept us all in line; she gave us all the love we needed. She baked all of our favorite goodies; gosh, I hope she comes back.

As the day went on, all of us were just sitting watching television. My dad came in the living room and asked me to come sit and talk to them. I remember I got up and said, "Daddy, if Mom is gone, will she ever come back?"

He looked at me and said "I'm not sure." Then I asked Daddy where our baby sister was and he said, "She is with your mom." I was so confused; I could not understand why a mother would leave so many children and a husband.

I also thought, *why would a mother take one child and not all of them?* I went into the kitchen and sat down next to my daddy, when my uncle Max started telling my sisters and myself that we are going to have to work together to help Daddy. Then I remember they kept talking to Lisa and Lilly. I guess because they were the oldest at home. I kept looking at Lisa and Daddy, and my mind kept racing from one thing to another. I couldn't even hear what they were all saying. I thought, *how are we going to pitch in to do all of our own washing?* We never did our own washing before. How are we going to cook and clean? I knew we didn't know how, we didn't even know how to make our own lunches for school… I just kept thinking to myself, *How are we going to do all this without Mom?*

Everything seemed so overwhelming, I couldn't even think straight. I just wanted to go to sleep and pray that this was just a nightmare. That night was so lonely without our mom; all of us were so confused. We could not understand what could be so bad to make our own mother leave all of us.

I remember the little ones kept asking Lisa for Mom. I felt so bad for them. When we told them she left, I remember Michael started crying and wanted us to take him to her. Then I remember I had seen Michael sitting on the sofa just looking out the window. I know he was looking for his mom to come home to him. Sandra and Ralphy kept crying and crying for mom. It hurt my heart so bad to see them ache for their mother. I kept thinking that the little ones never even spent the night away from Mom before. I thought to myself, *how are they going to be all right without their Mom?* I don't really know if the little ones knew if Mom was gone for good or just for a few days. I don't really think that they understood the difference, or any of this.

All of the emotions were really starting to get to Daddy. I saw Dad in his room, just sitting on his bed crying too. I just kept walking so that he would not see that I had seen him. I know now that his tears were for all of us. I went to the bathroom and I locked the door. I sat on the floor and just cried quietly to myself. I was so confused and no one had any answers for any of our questions—why would she leave all of us, and where was she, and could we call her?

I started praying for Mom to come back for me and for all of us. I started praying that I would try my best to be a better daughter, if she were to just come back home to all of us and to Daddy! I remember feeling very frightened for Mom; I often wondered if she was okay. I kept thinking of the look on my older sisters' faces when we were sitting at the table with Daddy and our uncles. I knew my sister Lisa was trying her best to comfort the little ones. But I think it was too big of a job for her. I tried my best to go to sleep, but I could hear Lisa crying and I knew Sandra was too.

I shared rooms with Lilly at the time, and I think Lilly was mad at Mom for doing this to us and to Daddy. Even though I had seen Lilly crying, I knew she was mad at Mom for doing this to all of us. I wanted to talk to Lisa, but she seemed so upset, I didn't want to upset her more. We were just a bunch of frightened and confused children. I couldn't think of anything worse than knowing that our own mother just picked up and left all of us without a second thought to what she was doing to any of us.

The days were so long and lonely without our Mom there. I hated going home after school without Mom there. It was so quiet and we never smelled goodies in the kitchen when we walked in from school, like before. I felt so sorry for my little brothers and my little sister. I knew they had to have been hurting very badly, because I was so torn inside. I kept looking at them and I could tell they missed Mom terribly. I knew they needed their Mommy; they needed her hugs and her kisses they needed their MOM BACK!!

Every day was a challenge for all of us to function without Mom. My aunts and uncles were trying to teach us chores and tasks to make things easier for us. We would come home from school and look at the schedule my aunts would make up for all of us to follow. Lisa cleaned the kitchen and tried her best to cook for us. I guess Mom had shown her a few dishes to make, because Lisa would cook and we liked it. Lisa always checked our homework now that Mom left. If we didn't understand, she would sit with us and help me and the little ones. I remember I had seen Lisa combing Sandra's hair. Then when she was done I seen her tell the boys to brush their teeth. I then thought to myself,"Gosh she is doing a great job with all of us and she is just in the ninth grade." I was so proud of my sister and I know daddy was too.

A lot of times, I think the kids felt as much love from their older sister as they did from Mom. Lilly would clean our room and the living room, and I would clean the bathroom. I remember Lisa would go into our parents' room and make the bed and straighten up. She always seemed to do more than what was on the schedule. My daddy started giving all of us lunch money for school, since Mom wasn't there anymore to make all of our lunches. That was so different. I was so used to Mom's lunches; I never got full or liked the school lunches. The school didn't have cooks or anything like that.

Different mothers would volunteer time during lunch in the cafeteria. On Mondays, the cafeteria would serve hot dogs or chili cheese dogs; on Tuesdays, they served sloppy joes; on Wednesdays, we had spaghetti; on Thursdays, we had cheeseburgers; and on Fridays were tuna sandwiches. The school didn't sell chips or anything to go with the sandwiches. But the school did sell milk, white or chocolate. After a while, I began to hate the lunches. Dad would have Lisa buy us chips and a pack of cookies or something sweet just to get us full.

I felt so sorry for my daddy; he never really took care of the inside of the house or all of us without Mom before, and I knew this was very overwhelming for him. He used to walk around the house in the mornings, getting ready for work or a meeting. I always saw a smile with a cry at the same time when I looked at Daddy. A lot of mornings, I remember going to church and praying to God to help Dad and all of us .I prayed for God to bring our mother home to us. I knew one day God would answer all of my prayers, to have my family together again.

I loved to see Dad in a good mood. It made me think maybe we would be okay now. I remember he would whistle and sing in the morning before he went out to a meeting or something. Daddy sang very well; so did his family. I used to love to hear them sing together. He tried so hard to cheer us all up, especially now that we were getting so close to Thanksgiving. But I still saw all the pain in his smile and in his eyes.

I remember waking up at night and waiting on the chair in the living room for Daddy to come home from work. When he finally came, it was always very late. Daddy would wake me and tell me to go lie down in my bed. I just wanted to see him and make sure that he came home; I guess I was afraid that one day he would leave all of us too. Daddy always worked so much. I guess he had to, with so many children and going to Catholic school. I knew was very expensive.

It seemed like everyone knew at school and at church that Mom had left all of us. They always seemed to look at us with pity in their eyes. Many times I felt very grateful, but sometimes I felt angry. I didn't want anyone's pity; I just wanted our mom back. Many nights I saw Daddy crying while he was in the kitchen or even just walking by while we were all lying on the living room floor watching television. I remember one night I heard Daddy say, "Even a dog don't leave her puppies." I never really knew what he meant by that saying, but I know I heard it over and over again through my childhood. I would turn around and look at him and he would just keep walking, while he would repeat himself by saying, "Even a dog don't leave her puppies." I remember that so many times it would hurt when I would hear him, but I would try to think of this statement as part of his pain too.

4

I think it was very hard for Daddy to look at us and think how could Mom do this to all of us, but at the same time, I know he was torn inside for all of us. Daddy always tried to cheer us up. Many Friday's daddy came home with pizza, shrimp or hamburgers. I always thought that was a loving gesture for daddy to do. Every time he did this Lisa didn't have to cook, which was great for Lisa. I know sometimes daddy blamed himself for mom leaving. I know he felt guilty, but now as a grown woman, I know it wasn't anyone's fault but our mother's. I had thought to myself," am I ever going to be able to forget all of the pain my mom has given all of her children?" Several weeks went by and we were really struggling just to get by without Mom. I think all of the older ones were feeling helpless not to be able to come up with some kind of solution to our family's problem.

My older brother Louis would come by pretty often and check on all of us. I really looked forward in seeing him; he would take all the little ones to the beach and to the park with his wife and daughter. I was always so happy to spend time with them. Louis would come by when he could, to drive us to school. I always thought that was pretty cool of him to do for all of us. When I would get out of his van, I would lean over to hug him and he looked at me so sadly, I knew he was hurting for all of us too. I walked away from his van thinking to myself, *Thank you, Jesus for my brother.*

Willie called pretty often from out of state. I guess Daddy must have told him about Mom leaving. Willie called one day from out of state, and he asked to speak to me. When I got on the phone, he asked me if Sandra and I wanted to go to his house and stay with my sister-in-law and my nephew. I was so excited; I asked Sandra and she started jumping up and down and said "yes." Willie told me to get a few outfits for me and Sandra, and that Carol would be picking us up soon. I asked him if it was all right with Daddy and he said, "Yes, Daddy knows. He said it was fine."

We were so excited; it was always fun to go to Willie and Carol's house. Carol was always very nice to us and we really loved her. I always felt like she was my real sister and not my sister-in-law. Carol would take us places and take us to her mom's house too. Her mom lived just two houses from Willie and Carol's house, so we would walk over to play with her two sisters. I loved playing with them. They were always so nice to Sandra and me. Carol's mom was also really sweet to us. I remember she was really crafty; she made different kinds of pottery. Her name was Mrs. Perez. She would invite us in her little workshop and show us how she worked. I was always so interested in her work. Sometimes when I felt Mrs. Perez hug me it almost felt like Mom's hugs.

I always enjoyed being with my sister-in-law and her family. I knew this was one of Willie's ways of helping Daddy. We loved it. I think we felt like a family again. Sometimes I felt like Mom was still at home, just waiting for me and Sandra to come home after our visit with Carol and Wick. Even though Willie was not in town for our visit with Carol and our nephew Wick, I still enjoyed going over to spend time with them.

I think we took turns going different places on the weekends because Daddy was gone so much. Lisa and Lilly were always with our cousins or their friends. Michael and Ralphy would be with different cousins or with Daddy during some weekends. It was getting harder and harder for all of us going from one relative's home to another. You see, Daddy traveled a lot, and even with all of this to deal with, he still had to leave. He went to Florida and New York quite often. I also remember him going to Georgia and Las Vegas.

Daddy was well known, and he was respected by everyone who knew him. I always wondered how he was able to do his work and be a mother and father to all of us too. I missed him so much when he left. But no matter what, I knew Daddy would come back to us. He always bought us so many souvenirs from so many different places. That was cool when he walked in the house and all of us would run up to him and kiss him on the cheek. He would laugh and give us his big garment bag. We knew what that meant. We would grab it from him and unzip the huge zipper and sure enough, all of our toys and goodies from his trip would fall out. He would buy so many things for each of us; he never forgot anyone or bought more for one of us and not all of us.

When my father went to New York I remember he would bring little models of the Statue of Liberty. Then when he went to Las Vegas he brought us little slot machines that held real money. I even saw things in his bag for our aunts and cousins too. Times like this, I would look at Daddy and think, *He's so great and we are too, why did Mom leave us and why hasn't she come back?*

Gosh I was really starting to get mad with Mom for doing this to all of us. Time was going by and Mom still hadn't come home. I could tell it was getting harder and harder without Mom. My aunts and uncles and my grandparents were all pitching in helping Daddy and us. My aunt Janie, my father's sister, would take us up to her home in Houston. We always liked going there. She didn't have any children, and I always knew she would have been a great mother. She loved Daddy so much; I could see it in her face when she hugged all of us.

My aunt Olivia is my father's baby sister; she has five kids and we loved playing with her kids. She would come over with her husband, my uncle "Hoss" and take us to her home to spend the night. My uncle Hoss is so handsome; I always thought he looked like a movie star. I loved spending time with them; they were always so nice and loving with all of us. All of them took turns with two or three of us at a time when Daddy had to go out of town on a convention. My aunt Olivia and my uncle Hoss took care of my father's parents. My grandmother and grandfather lived there with them all my life. Even with all the kids, my aunt had and my grandparents to care for. My aunt still would take a few of us at a time to help Daddy. I knew she must really love her brother to do all of this. I loved seeing all the love they had for each other.

I remember looking at my aunts and seeing such pain in their faces for their brother. I really felt everyone loved Daddy so much that they wanted to help him make this horrible situation easier. But I don't think anyone had a solution to our problems.

As time went on, I started noticing Michael was getting very quiet. I asked him one day if there was anything I could do to cheer him up. Michael looked at me and said, "Ruthie, I just want Mom to come back. I miss her too much and I want her back."

I started to cry and I told him, "Michael, she will come back. I know she must miss us as much as we miss her." Michael was so sad; it hurt me to see him like that. When Daddy came home that night, I waited up for him. I heard his car pulling in the driveway. I looked out the window and I saw Daddy getting out of his car. He looked so tired and so sad.

I opened the door and I said, "Hi, Daddy." He looked at me and smiled, then bent down for me to kiss him on the cheek. You see, Daddy always would put his cheek out for us to kiss him. I loved him so much and I loved kissing his cheek.

When he went inside, he put his hat on the coffee table and I said, "Daddy, Michael was real sad today. He kept crying for Mom."

Daddy looked at me and said, "Even a dog don't leave her puppies." Then he just walked towards the kitchen. I kind of brushed the comment off.

Then I looked at him and said, "Daddy, can't you call Mom or something just so that Michael and all of us will feel better?"

Daddy just looked at me for a few seconds and said "I told you, honey, I don't know where your mom is or how to get a hold of her."

I just looked at him. I felt so lost; I couldn't understand any of this and why would Mom not leave a number or some way for us to contact her? I started thinking, *What if something happens to one of us? How will Mom know or will she try to see us or call us?*

Daddy came in the living room and told me, "Ruthie, it's late; you need to get to bed."

I didn't want to go to bed, I wanted to help my brother so that he would not be sad anymore. But I looked over to my father and said, "Okay Daddy, good night." As I was walking up the stairs, I saw Daddy walking towards Michael and Ralphy's room. I knew he felt bad for Michael; that's why he was walking towards their room. I peeked around the doorway and saw Daddy kissing them both on their foreheads. I knew Daddy wanted to make them feel better; he just didn't know how.

I felt so bad for all of us and for Daddy that I just quietly went upstairs and tried my best to go to sleep for school the next day. My chest started hurting me from the pain of my family. I felt so bad for my family but I didn't know what to do to help them.

5

The next day was kind of rough. Lisa was getting the little ones ready for school and telling Lilly and me to eat something. We were all ready and Lisa and Lilly started out to school, and Ralphy, Michael, Sandra, and I were right behind them walking to school. Lisa gave all of us our lunch money and told us to be careful and to go straight to school and straight back. We always did what she told us and we knew she would somehow know if we stopped on the way. It seemed like everyday was such a challenge for each of us. Gosh I was so lost.

I really missed Sundays when we would all get together with our families at our house. Mom would cook or Daddy would barbeque. It was always so much fun with all my aunts, uncles, and cousins. They would laugh and sing while all the kids just played and played. My grandmother Ruth and her husband with their adopted son would come over every Sunday too. This was my mom's mother. I am named also after my grandmother and my great-grandmother. I was the fourth Ruthie.

My Mom's family was kind of strange. I always thought that to myself. I really never understood, but we called my grandmother's husband "Jesse," instead of calling him "Grandpa." My mom's parents were divorced, and both of them remarried when my mom was still in high school. All of us called my step-grandmother "Grandma Nena." But Jesse was always Jesse to all of us...

I remember our step-grandmother was such a loving grandmother; we all loved her very much. My mom's dad who is our grandpa Charlie was a great grandpa. We all loved him so much also... My grandfather used to be a boxer when he was younger. I always thought that was pretty cool. Our grandfather Charlie and our step grandmother Nena were like the perfect grandparents any kid would love to have. But on the other hand my grandmother Ruth and Jesse were just plain strange. We really didn't think Jesse liked any of us. He never hugged us or even so much to say hi. My grandmother Ruth was kind of weird too. She would travel to different places, and when she came over on Sundays, she always put presents for us in our clothes dryer. Then she would leave and all of the kids would run to the dryer and open it to see what she bought for us. I always thought she was weird for doing that. But we kind of thought Jesse didn't know of the gifts she bought all of us. So we always kept her little secret. She always made weird comments to each of us. She always said things that were kind of insulting. I just brushed them off since we were not that close with them. I always thought she just wanted Mom to herself and she didn't like the idea that Mom had so many kids.

After years went by, we really didn't question it or think too much of it. When she and Jesse came over, they would bring their adopted son Tony over with them. He was older than me. I think he was around 16 years old when I was 12. I started hating when they came over. The year I turned twelve was when I seen the real Tony. No one knew, but every time all the kids played hide and seek, Tony would hide by me and touch me. At first he would act like it was an accident. Then I don't think he really cared what I thought of him. I think Tony just wanted to touch me any chance he could. I remembered I cried, but I was afraid to tell anyone. I remember the first time he touched me. I was hiding on the side of the house and he came to hide right by me. Then I felt his hand in the back of my shorts, touching my butt. I turned around and looked at him then I told him to stop it or I was going to tell my older brother.

He said to me, "So what, they won't believe you anyway!" I was mad but I was also scared. That day, I could not wait for my grandmother, Tony and Jesse to leave. I never said anything to anyone. I guess I was afraid to.

I really hated when they came over. It seemed like every chance Tony got to touch me, he would. I sometimes wish I could have told Mom. But I know now that if she could leave all her children and not protect them from harm, then why did I think she would have helped me? Now that Mom left, my grandmother kept coming over every Sunday. Every Sunday that meant Tony came over too.

I heard my Grandma Ruth telling my Daddy she didn't know where my Mom was or how to contact her. She kept saying, "Luis maybe she will call me." When they came over, I stayed inside. I told Lilly and Michael I just didn't feel like playing. Tony knew it was because of him why I didn't want to go outside and play.

I thought to myself that if my life was now upside down with Mom gone, why should I put up with Tony touching me? I was just a little girl. He had no right touching me. So I stayed inside where I knew I was safe. There were many times I wanted to tell my mom's brother, my uncle Memo. My uncle is my mom's only sibling from my two grandparents. Then, when my grandfather and my step-grandmother got married, they had many children together. My uncle's name is William, just like my brother. We called him Memo which is short for William in Spanish.

I loved my uncle and I knew my uncle loved me. I remember one year, my uncle and his wife, my aunt Janie, bought me a bike for my birthday. The bike was red with a small white basket on it. My uncle took me outside to teach me how to ride my new bike, and Tony came over and ran right into me and I fell. My uncle scolded Tony and told him to go play with the older kids. I was bleeding on my knee but at the same time, I was so happy to hear my uncle scolding him.

I kept thinking to myself, *Should I tell my uncle, and if I do, what will he do and what will Tony do?* That day, I wanted so badly to tell him what Tony was doing to me, but I was so afraid to. I wasn't sure what would happen if I got Tony into trouble. Many times after Mom left when my uncle came over, I wanted to tell him. I knew if he knew, he would help me and put a stop to all the touching Tony was doing. I don't understand why I was so frightened to tell someone. Deep down I know one of my brothers would have beat his butt if they knew what he had done to me all this time. I was just too embarrassed to tell I guess. I just thought to myself that I would stay far away from Tony as possible. I just could not get the courage to tell someone. I didn't want to worry Daddy or anyone else during this hard time in our lives…

Every Sunday when Grandma Ruth came over, I always had the feeling she knew where Mom was. But then I would see her crying with Daddy and think that there was no way she could know… If she did, I was sure she would help us bring her back. I remember about a year or so before my mom left us, my grandmother and Jesse were fighting and Jesse hit my grandmother. My grandmother had a black eye and a busted lip from the fight.

Then my mom told the girls that my grandmother and Tony were going to stay with us awhile. I hated to hear that because I knew Tony would try to touch me again, and even more since they would be staying overnight. Tony and my grandmother had never stayed the night before, so I felt myself really getting scared. One night I went to bed and my grandmother was in the bathroom. I heard the water running, so I knew she was taking a bath. I wondered where Tony was, and then I heard a noise. I looked into the hallway from my bed and I saw Tony looking through the keyhole of the bathroom door at my grandmother while she was taking a bath. It seemed like he was watching her forever.

I then started getting really frightened, thinking to myself that he was really sick. First he was touching me, and then he was watching his own mom take a bath. But then it dawned on me that my grandmother was not Tony's real mother. I remembered that Tony was adopted. Either way, I still thought he was a pervert for watching my grandmother take a bath. As I was lying there in my bed, Sandra was right on the other side of me. Then I heard my grandmother shut off the water. I then felt a jump on the bed. I was afraid to look behind me. Then I felt his hand on my butt. He started rubbing me and running his fingers up and down my crack. I was so frightened, I started crying, and he whispered to me to be quiet. As I was lying there being touched and violated as a little girl, I then started hating my life. I prayed for him to stop. I wanted so badly for Daddy or one of my brothers to catch him doing this to me.

I felt him touching himself while he was touching me. I wanted so much to jump up and run out of there but I knew if I did, he would be alone with Sandra. I didn't want him touching or hurting my little sister. I then heard my grandmother getting out of the bathroom. I thanked God for her getting out of the bathroom so fast. She came over to the bed and Tony was acting like he was asleep.

She then said, "Tony, let's go to bed in the other room." She didn't even think it was odd for him to be lying on the same bed and in between Sandra and myself. I thought that finally now I could go to sleep without him in my bed. That night I prayed for them to go back to their own house. I hated Tony being there every day. Then, after a few days, I saw Jesse had come to our house. I was so happy; I knew he was coming to take them back home with him. He started talking to Daddy and Mom and then I saw my grandmother Ruth getting all of their things together to go home.

I wanted to jump up and down and say to them, "Leave and don't come back even if you get hit again." I knew then that Tony watches my grandmother on a daily basis while she's bathing and dressing. Then when he needs something different, he touches me on Sundays when they come over. Gosh I really hated him.

Now that Mom was gone, I wished they would just stay away from all of us. It wasn't like they were helping us or helping Daddy with our horrible situation anyway. My grandmother never even offered to help Daddy with any of us. I kind of thought it was because of Jesse that she never offered. That was okay with me; I didn't want to go over to their house anyway. I was so happy when I watched all three of them drive off... I knew my brothers really didn't like Tony very much. They used to make fun of him and say he was a sissy. He used to wear white shiny dress shoes all the time with white pants and a white jacket. Gosh, I hated him. He had everyone fooled. He had dark brown hair and he parted it on the side. My brothers used to say he was a nerd and a sissy. But they really didn't know that he was a pervert too. I never even saw my brothers hang out with him. I think Tony didn't want to be around my brothers. It seemed like he was always around the girls. I just wanted him to stay away from me.

The touching didn't seem to last too long after Mom had left us. Sometimes I wondered if Tony knew that mom was not happy with all of us, and maybe that is why he took advantaged of our situation. So in every way I felt relieved that Tony wasn't coming over as often. Christmas was getting closer and Mom still had not called us or come back home. I was really starting to get scared about Mom's well-being. We were getting ready to go to our grandpa's and our step-grandmother's house for a few days. I really loved going to their house and pretending that they are my parents. Daddy was going to a convention to New York. My older sisters were going to our Aunt Olivia's house; they really liked it over there. I knew that was good for Lisa, since she had so much responsibility. This kind of gave Lisa a break. Now my two sisters could rest from all of us.

Michael and Ralph were going to our Uncle Max's house. Sandra and I went to our grandpa's and our grandma Nena's home. I enjoyed going to our family's homes but I hated being separated from the little ones. Everyone was always so nice and loving to all of us; I knew they loved all of us, but I also knew how much they loved their brother. I don't know what we would have done if we didn't have such a great and supportive family and I was glad we did.

I could tell Grandpa was ashamed of what Mom did to all of us. I heard him talking one day, saying that he was going to disown Mom even though she was his own daughter. Grandpa and Grandma Nena still were there for all of us and for our father. I remember when Sandra and I stayed over; our grandpa gave us our lunch money. Then before we walked out to the car my grandma gave us lunch money also. My aunt Cindy was Sandra's age and my uncle David was my age. They both would laugh and they told us that they liked when we went over to their house because they always got double lunch money from their parents. They were so funny. I always forgot all of my problems when we stayed over at our grandparent's home.

I really loved them for always being there for all of us. I also know my daddy was always grateful for all of their love and support.

The day Daddy came back we were so happy to see him and each other. Daddy always seemed so happy to see all of us too. He went from relative to relative's house to pick us all up. I saw him smile and his eyes started getting watery after every pickup. I felt so bad for him; he was hurting so much for all of us and himself...

I knew that things had to get better, they just had to. Well, Christmas came and we were not very excited to open our presents. Daddy and Lisa picked us up so many neat toys. But the little ones and I just didn't look happy. I know that we just wanted our mom back. Daddy and Lisa decorated the tree for Christmas; it was a big white one with blue ornaments that Mom had picked out for our family from last Christmas. We always had such a nice tree for Christmas. It was so hard trying to celebrate Christmas and all holidays without Mom there.

6

Shortly after all the holidays, I remember Lisa and Lilly had gone to a dance. Daddy would let them go with our cousins or their friends since they helped so much around the house and with the little ones. They loved going to dances. Both sisters danced very well, so I know they really enjoyed it. That night, Ralph, Sandra, Michael, and I were lying down on the living room floor. I think we fell asleep while we were watching television. Then daddy came in and woke me up. I looked up at him and said, "Yes Daddy, what's wrong?"

Daddy told me to go check the upstairs and see if one of the girls left any incense or candles lit. Daddy said he could smell something burning. I ran upstairs to look. When I got to the top of the stairs, I could smell smoke. I looked in Lisa's room and saw that the whole room was on fire. I ran down the stairs and told Daddy.

I said, "Daddy, Daddy, the upstairs is all on fire." Daddy told me to get all the kids together and go outside by the street. I saw Daddy walking towards the phone. I knew he was calling the fire department. I then woke up the little ones. By the time we got outside, I heard the fire trucks coming. Very shortly after, I saw my uncle Max. He got out of his car and ran over to us and asked us if we were all right. We told him we were fine. Before I knew it, my other uncles were there as well. I saw my uncle Jesse and my uncle Tony. Then I saw my uncle Max walk over to hug Daddy. Uncle Max was such a great uncle but he was an even greater brother. He stayed right next to Daddy the whole time until the fire department put out the fire.

All of us watched in fear as the firemen threw all the furniture out of Lisa's bedroom window. I really started to feel sad and scared. I knew that we lost a lot of our things, if not all of our things. I looked around and saw all of our things on the front lawn. Gosh, that night was so devastating to me. I was just so thankful that no one got hurt. That night, all of us stayed at our uncle Max's house. We were pretty sad the next day when we saw the damage that the fire had done. The fire ruined all of the girls' things, even all of our uniforms for school. We went to school wearing regular clothes that Lisa had washed for us that day. I was so sad that all of our toys, pictures, and special things were now gone.

I prayed that night to God to help us through all this, and asked why bad things kept happening to all of us. I knew things were getting very rough for my father. As time went on, I could tell that all my dad's family wanted to help Daddy with all of us, but there was just so much that we needed. The main thing we needed was for Mom to come home… We needed our mom to comfort the little ones and to let them know everything would be all right But I knew that wasn't going to happen.

A few days went by and I heard the phone ring. All the people from the insurance company were there fixing and renovating all the damage from the fire. I ran to answer the phone and right when I said hello, I heard a voice saying, "Ruthie, it's me, Mom."

I froze, then I started crying and I said, "Mom, where are you? We miss you. When are you coming back?"

Mom asked me if everyone was okay from the fire and I told her yes. She didn't answer any of my questions that I asked her. Then I saw Daddy walk inside. I looked over at him and said, "Daddy, its Mom."

Daddy looked confused and angry when he heard what I said. He walked over to me, took the phone, and started talking to Mom. I could not understand what they were saying. Daddy was speaking in Spanish. The adults always spoke Spanish when they were speaking to each other, so that the children could not understand them..

A little later, Daddy hung up the phone. I walked into his room and I asked him if Mom was coming back. Daddy looked at me and said, "No." I didn't dare to ask anymore questions. I just turned around and went and sat on the front porch. I felt like Mom just didn't love any of us enough to come back and make sure we were all right.

I started wondering how she knew of the fire. How could she call and not come home? I knew now that Mom was okay, and I was never going to worry about her anymore. It's not like she was worrying about any of her children. Gosh, that was the moment that I was really starting to hate my very own mother.

When Lisa came home, I was sure Dad told her that Mom called today. A little later, Lisa walked outside to where I was sitting. She then sat right next to me then she asked me what Mom said. I told her that I asked her when she was coming home and she didn't answer me. Then mom had asked me if everyone was okay from the fire. I told her yes and that's when Daddy walked in and I told him it was Mom on the phone. That was all I knew. After that, Daddy was speaking in Spanish to her and then they hung up. Lisa told me Mom wasn't coming back. I could tell Lisa started getting real mad at Mom for leaving all of us and leaving her with so much work and responsibility. I was really starting to feel very bad for my sister. Lisa did so much work to help Dad with all of us and the house. There were so many days when we didn't want to listen to her; I can only imagine how frustrating that must have been for Lisa. My poor sister was still stuck with being a Mom and sister to all of us. That day I just watched everyone that I love in silence.

After a while, we started hearing things from our cousins about Mom. A few of our cousins were saying that they heard my uncles and aunts say, that Mom was with our cousin Arturo. I questioned them, asking where they were, and why Mom would be with him. They really didn't know any details of her whereabouts. They kept saying that this is what my father's family thought. That night, I asked Lisa if Mom was with Arturo and where they were. Lisa told me she heard the same thing. Lisa started telling me that she heard from our cousins that Mom and Arturo were a couple, and that he never went back to his mom's house after he left our house.

I asked Lisa how could Mom leave all of us for him. Lisa looked at me and said, "I don't know, but I know one thing: he is Daddy's cousin and Mom is so wrong doing this. Lisa looked at me and said, "I hate her, Ruthie. I hate what she's doing to all of us and to Daddy."

We then started crying and we just hugged each other. I started thinking of the months that Arturo lived with us. I started remembering how he and Mom would act around each other. I do remember she would make him a good meal and they would walk to the grocery stores together. Arturo always pushed the basket of groceries all the way home for Mom. I remember seeing all his favorite items in the grocery cart just like Lilly said. I remember Daddy would come home real late and get his dinner out of the oven where Mom would put it, and it was always a burrito. But for dinner Arturo would eat a steak with vegetables and potatoes. I thought to myself that all that time Lilly suspected something was not right between mom and Arturo and she was right. I wondered how long they were seeing each other.

I know that's why Lilly hated him so much; I think she knew that Mom was giving Arturo special treatment over Daddy. I recall even when Mom had our baby sister Patricia; I saw a huge vase with three cupids on it. It was like a pearl color. I never saw such a beautiful vase in all my life. There had to have been at least two dozen roses in the vase. I asked my mom if Daddy bought them for her and she said, "Oh no, Arturo bought them for me. Aren't they beautiful?" I really didn't think too much of it at that time; I always thought he was just grateful to our parents for all they had done for him.

Then I remember seeing Mom dancing with Arturo at our cousin's wedding. Now that I think about it, that jerk was seeing our mother right under Daddy's nose and right under all of our noses as well. Gosh, Dad's family must be pretty mad to know what he did, even after all the help everyone gave his stupid ass.

Well, things started getting really bad around the house. I think my family all knew that Mom was with Arturo; they just didn't know where… Daddy never really told us what they suspected, but we all knew from our cousins. I was kind of embarrassed because I always thought of Mom as a good mother and wife. How could a good Mom leave all her children and her husband for her husband's very own young cousin? This is the same cousin that my father helped out with a job and let live in his house. I know my father didn't think in a million years that his own family would do something like this to him. All of my father's family has been married for many years to the same person. How could this happen to such a great family? I told myself that if all of this is true I don't ever want to speak to my mother again. But I also knew that I have to see the facts or hear this from my father to believe it. I guess I will just wait and see if my father will talk to any of us about what they suspect.

One day, a social worker came to our home, wanting to speak to Daddy. We told her that Daddy was at work. The social worker started asking a lot of questions, wanting to know who watches us and who cooks and cleans for us while Daddy is at work. I told her to come back and speak to my father later when he was home. I also told her that everyone in our family pitched in to help all of us when Daddy worked. She left her card and said for me to have Daddy call her. I felt scared, not knowing what was going to happen next. I couldn't wait for Lisa or one of my older siblings to come home so that I could tell them about the social worker.

Daddy was working; I knew he would not be home until that night. But I knew Lisa would know what to do with this information. Finally, Lisa came home and we told her about the lady who came over. Lisa didn't seem too concerned, so I didn't worry about it any longer. When Daddy came home, Lisa told him about the social worker. I heard Daddy tell Lisa that he would take care of it, and not to worry.

Daddy spoke to his brothers and sisters and tried to fix our problem I guess they decided to help daddy even more during the day than before… I asked Daddy why that social worker was asking so many questions and he said they wanted an adult to be with all of us when he was at work. I told Dad that Lisa was always with all of us. I told him we were never by ourselves. Daddy told us that the social worker said Lisa was still a teenager and we needed an adult there with us. I asked him what they would do if Lisa watched us, and he said," nothing; there is nothing they can do." After that, Dad just looked at me and said "Don't worry about it, everything will be all right." But I knew they were going to try to take us from Daddy. I think my dad just didn't want to scare us. But I also knew Daddy would not let anyone hurt us or separate us from him.

I thought to myself, *Great, one more thing for Daddy to worry about.* The next day, my grandmother came over to stay with us while Daddy was working. We really didn't speak too much to my grandmother; she only spoke Spanish. But she sure knew how to show us she loved us, even without speaking. My grandmother is Daddy's mother. She was very short and petite. She had very long salt-and- pepper hair, always worn in a bun on top of her head. She was very good to all of us. I always wanted to be able to speak to her. I knew she was a very loving woman and with her being here with us, I knew the little ones really missed our mother even more.

Daddy had so much to worry about. I knew all of this was really getting to him. I remember he came home one night and he walked by my room saying, "Even a dog don't leave her puppies." I picked my head up off my pillow to look at him. Daddy just kept on walking towards his room. I turned over and just cried. I thought I was crying for myself, but now I know I was crying for all of us, including Daddy.

The months came and went, and we still did not hear another word from Mom. My grandmother Ruth stopped coming over. I heard from one of my cousins that Daddy told my grandmother he knew that she knew where our Mom was. They also told me that my grandmother Ruth told my mom that our house caught on fire. It all seemed to add up about how Mom knew about the fire. I thought to myself, *all this time she came to our house and cried saying she didn't know why Mom would leave and she didn't know where she was.* I didn't care even if she did know. I just knew if Daddy was mad at her then that's great. That means if she doesn't come visit anymore then Tony won't come either!

I thought to myself, *now I will never be touched again!* I was so happy. I wasn't even sad about probably never seeing my grandmother Ruth again. I think at times I blamed my grandmother for adopting Tony and bringing him into our lives. That was the last time I had ever seen Tony. I really thanked God for answering my prayers and for getting him out of my life. So was I sad about not seeing my grandmother and Tony? Heck NO!

7

Everyone was helping all of us and Daddy. On Sundays, we were still going to church and Daddy would still help out in the church cafeteria making tamales. Daddy worked so hard, I hardly ever saw him rest. One of the ladies who worked in the cafeteria at the church started coming over to our home to help Daddy with all of us. I guess Daddy had to make sure an adult was with us at all times, and he did. Whenever Daddy had to work or go out of town, he always made sure someone was there to watch all of us. Time went on and I never heard of that social worker coming over to our home again.

We never went to the beach anymore as a family either. We went to the beach with our older brothers or with our aunts and uncles. But never with Daddy anymore. I guess it was too hard for him with mom gone. That was something we did as a family with Mom. I really missed being a family. I hated what Mom did to all of us. I could tell it was killing Daddy inside, knowing that his wife left him and all her children for his very own cousin.

I thought of Daddy not seeing his baby daughter. I also thought that it was so hard on Daddy knowing my mom had his daughter with her and his own cousin. I often wondered if my baby sister thought that my cousin Arturo was her Daddy. I couldn't think of anyone who had such a horrible situation in their own family other than ours. I went to school and things just were just not the same. I always had to explain to my friends why my mom was no longer a room mother or why she never came to help out anymore.

My friend Kim Martinez had been my friend since kindergarten. Kim lived with her grandmother and grandfather. During the months Arturo lived with us, I remember Mom would let me stay at Kim's house to spend the night. Many times, she even let Sandra stay with me over there. It was always so much fun; Kim's grandparents would take us to the ice skating rink in Houston to skate. We always loved going over there. Now that Mom had left us, sometimes I looked at how much Kim loved her grandmother and thought to myself, *Can I leave Daddy and go live with my grandfather and step-grandmother?*

But sometimes I guess I just wanted to be with a mother figure. I always felt that I couldn't hurt Daddy by leaving him too. I think Kim's grandmother must have talked with Daddy about letting Sandra and me go to their home, because Kim's house was the only place Sandra and I ever stayed at overnight other than with our families at their homes. I kind of wondered if that's why Mom let me go to Kim's house so much. Mom even let us spend the night during school nights at Kim's house. I think she let us because I was old enough to understand that she was seeing Arturo behind my father's back. She knew I would have noticed what her and Arturo were doing while my father was working.

Kim never asked me anything about Mom leaving us. I kind of think that's why I really got so close with her, because she didn't want to hurt my feelings by talking about my family's situation. I remember when Kim's grandmother dropped us off at school; she would lean over and hug Sandra and me right after hugging Kim. She always made me feel so loved, even more so now without my own Mom there. I really loved Kim's grandmother. I felt the same amount of love for her as I did my very own step-grandmother. This always made me take a real look at my own mother's actions. Gosh, my mom was such a bitch for doing this to us!!!

My family that was so perfect is more torn now than when my mom first left us. I promised myself that I would try not to think of Mom or think of her being with Arturo. So I tried my best to accept the fact that my mom didn't love any of us enough to come back to us.

One day, to our surprise, we walked in from school and my aunt Janie was visiting. We were always so happy to see her. My aunt Janie was my daddy's sister. Her husband was our uncle Bruce. Uncle Bruce and Aunt Janie were so nice to all of us. I always remembered that we always had so much fun with Aunt Janie. Uncle Bruce was so smart; we could ask him anything we wanted and he would answer us with such detail. I always felt like I would learn something new at every visit. My aunt Janie and my uncle Bruce really loved each other too. I really enjoyed watching them together. They were so funny too. They had nicknames for a few of us. Aunt Janie called Sandra a word in Spanish, and when I asked her what it meant, she said it meant "thumbtack" in English. I laughed when I heard this because Sandra was real small. So that nickname really went well with her.

My brother Hector loved going to their house in Houston. They were very close with all of us, but I knew Michael and Hector really liked it over there. They used to go pretty often when Mom was at home with us.

I ran up to Aunt Janie and said, "Hi, Aunt Janie! Are you staying with us today?"

She looked at me and smiled and said, "Yes I am, honey."

During Aunt Janie's stay, one day when we came home from school, I noticed we had new furniture. As I walked in, I asked Aunt Janie, "Did my daddy buy all this?"

Aunt Janie looked at me and said, "Yes he did, do you like it?"

I looked at her and smiled and said, "Yes I do."

We had a real fancy living room set and daddy even got a new bedroom set. We also had new fancy lamps with matching coffee tables for the living room. I asked Aunt Janie why we got new furniture when our other furniture was in excellent condition. Aunt Janie looked at me and said, "Well, I thought it would be easier on your daddy if I changed the furniture. Every day he comes in from work, everything is a touch of your mom and I thought if I changed the bedroom set and the living room set that he would not be in so much pain."

I thought that was nice of her to be so concerned with Daddy's feelings. I just went up to her and hugged her. I asked her if she thought that Mom thinks about us and misses us. She looked at me and said, "I think so; all of you are such a blessing. If you were my children, I could not stop thinking of any of you."

As I looked around me, I really started seeing how sad the little ones were. They seemed so lost without Mom. Aunt Janie tried her best to show us love, but I know the little ones needed their mother. My sisters were doing a lot of things with our cousins Belinda and Lydia. They were both my father's siblings' kids. While Sandra and I were spending more time with Kim's family or our grandpa and step grandma. We were all so very close. I could almost see the embarrassment on my family's faces when they were all together. I know it must have been so hard for them to not hate Mom for humiliating this great family the way she did.

I sometimes wondered, why didn't Mom leave Dad for some other man and not his very own cousin? I know that is what hurts. I could tell everyone was still in shock about Mom leaving all her children. This was the same woman who was such a great wife and mother. I guess we didn't really matter anymore to Mom. I felt that the only thing that mattered to Mom was Arturo and my baby sister. I started thinking that mom must have been really in love with Arturo for her to leave her home, all of her children and her husband. I don't think I could ever understand WHY?? Why did she do this to us and to daddy? I just wished that this was all a nightmare and that when I wakeup it will all go away. But I know it's not a nightmare it's my life.

A few weeks went by, and Michael, Sandra, Ralphy, and I were walking home from school. As we walked towards the back door of our house, we seen Daddy's car in the driveway. We started running towards the house because it wasn't every day we saw Daddy during the day. We got so excited that we started running towards the kitchen door the little ones were yelling," Daddy's home.". Just as we entered the kitchen, we saw Daddy. But much to our surprise, we also saw our Mom.

I thought to myself, *Thank you, Jesus, for bringing our mother back.* We ran up to Mom and started crying, and said "Mom, you're back, gosh we missed you so much. We are so glad to see you." We kept hugging her. Then I looked up and saw Daddy crying. I knew he was really happy for all of us.

I looked at the little ones and I could not help but cry for them. They were so excited to see Mom. Sandra kept hugging her, and Ralphy and Michael were touching any part of her they could reach. Mom really didn't seem as excited to see us as we were to see her. She hugged us and kissed us, but something seemed different; she seemed sad in a way. But I didn't care. I tried my best to not think negative. I was just glad to have our Mom back.

Mom didn't even explain anything to us about where she had been or who she was with. I looked at her and wondered why she left us in the first place. I thought to myself, *gosh, it was so hard without her.* Then I thought that I was just so glad she was back, I didn't care where she had been. I didn't even care if she was with Arturo. I was just glad she came to her senses. Her place was here with us, raising us and taking care of all her children.

I started thinking that now we could go back to being a happy family. The little ones kept hugging Mom; they were so happy to see her. Michael kept hugging her, and telling me," I told you mom would come back Ruthie I told you." I was so happy for them and myself. I thought, *now Lisa doesn't have to work so hard anymore. And we don't have to split up anymore when Daddy goes out of state.*

But Mom still seemed different; she didn't seem as loving or concerned about what we had been going through. She never said she was sorry for leaving all of us, or putting our family through so much turmoil. I really wished I had the courage to ask her why she hurt all of us so much and Daddy too. There was so much I wanted to say to her but I didn't. I guess I was afraid if I made her mad, she would leave again....

It was kind of weird with Mom back; she was so different. I really can't explain but she was not the same mom that I missed and loved so much. Mom kept making real bad comments about my father's family. I could not understand why she was so angry with all of them. I kept thinking of all the help all of them had given Daddy and all of us. I don't know what we would have done without all their love and support.

Then Mom walked into the kitchen and she made a phone call. I heard her ordering new furniture from the furniture store. While we were eating dinner, I was wondering why she would buy new furniture when we just got all of this furniture just a few weeks ago. My aunt Janie took a lot of time picking out this furniture. I could not understand why Mom wanted new furniture.

I asked Mom when she hung up the phone why we were getting new stuff. She just looked at me then she snapped at me and said, "This is all your Aunt Janie's taste. I don't like any of this." Then she looked into the living room and said, "That couch looks like a damn coffin." Mom then looked at me and said, "Do you like this ugly stuff?"

I just looked at her. I didn't even answer because I didn't see anything wrong with any of it. Then I asked her, "Mom, what are we going to do with all the stuff Aunt Janie picked out?"

Mom looked at me and smiled and said "I called the Goodwill. They are coming today to pick up all this junk."

I really started feeling confused and I thought to myself, *what the heck is going on? Why is Mom wasting Daddy's money on buying new furniture? My mom acts like my dad's family hurt her or us and it's the other way around.*

The next few days were kind of weird too. Mom and Dad slept in sleeping bags because the new furniture that Mom picked out had not been delivered yet. The Goodwill came and picked up all our other furniture that same day. My mom looked happy when they were carrying all the furniture out to their big truck.

Daddy seemed different too. He seemed sad still, even though Mom was back home. I could not understand why he still seemed sad with Mom back now. Then I realized that my aunts and uncles had not come by to visit us. They had not even so much as called our home. I think Mom must have told them something, because they would call every day to check on us. I guess Mom was still kind of angry with them. I just could not understand why.

I really didn't like the way we were not so close to everyone now that Mom was back. I started noticing Mom was asking a lot of questions about Dad's family. She started asking about who came over and who cleaned the house. Then she asked who went into her room when she was gone. She kept asking about our aunts and asking what they were doing, and what did they talk about when she was gone.

I looked at her and said, "Mom, they didn't ask me anything about you, and they never seemed like they were mad at you." I wished I could have been strong and said, "They are not like that to snoop into your things, the same things you left behind." I could not understand why she had so much hatred and anger towards them.

Mom was saying a lot of bad things about my uncles too. I kept wondering why she was so angry at my father's entire family. This was the same family that never even got angry at each other. The same family that would do anything for each other. The same family that helped us all this year that she had been gone! I started noticing that Mom seemed like she really didn't want to be there with us. When we left to school mom didn't walk us anymore I guess she figured that we walked by ourselves when she was gone so we can keep walking by ourselves. So many things were different. Mom never went to our school anymore to be a room mother either. I really feel that she just didn't want to be our mother anymore. I kept waiting for mom to explain why she left all of us. But my wait kept getting longer and longer. I don't think she will ever say," I am sorry for leaving all of you and I promise never to leave any of you again I love all of you with all my heart." My God I really want to hear her say that to me and to all of my brothers and sisters...

I kept seeing Mom talk on the phone, and when I would walk in, she would stop talking. I wondered who she was talking to but I just figured it was just adult things and none of my business. Mom always spoke in Spanish when she was on the phone. I kind of wondered if she was talking to Arturo. I knew he only spoke Spanish.

Then I tried my best to think positive about Mom. I thought to myself, *Mom wants to be here with us or she would have never come back to us!* But then Mom seemed angry at us every time she hung up the phone. I asked Lilly if she thought Mom was happy to be home with all of us.

Lilly looked at me and said, "Ruthie I know one thing: No matter what, Daddy would have NEVER LEFT US LIKE MOM DID!" Things were so different now that Mom came home. I don't recall any more goodies made in the kitchen by Mom. I guess she was still mad at Daddy. But I still couldn't understand why… In the mornings she made our lunches, but they were nothing like the lunches she used to make for all of us.

I guess it was going to take awhile for Mom to get used to being back home with a bunch of kids again. I saw her yell at Ralph one day and I wanted to get up and tell her something. I thought to myself, *He was just a little boy and his mommy left him with no explanation for a whole year.* I kept thinking how hard it must have been for Ralph because he was just in kindergarten at the time.. I could not imagine not having a Mom at only five years old. It was so hard for me and I was 12 years old when I got the news that my mother left me!

Ralphy looked at Mom almost like he was afraid of her. That day, I felt like I hated my own mother. I didn't want her to yell at Ralphy or any of us. Then, just as I looked up, I saw her spank him and she told him that he was spoiled. I looked at her and just ran to my room and cried. I wanted so much to hit her back for my little brother. I wished for Daddy to come home and stop her from being so mean to Ralphy. I then thought, *Is this a good thing that Mom came back?* I wished Lisa were at home. I know she would never let anyone hurt Ralphy not even Mom. I know that for sure.

For a whole year, that's all Lisa did was take care of all of us and protect us from anyone who would hurt us. Daddy was so proud of Lisa; I knew it, I could see it in his eyes when he hugged her. I was too. She was our mother and sister for a whole year. I guess everyone else was just happy Mom was back. But Mom herself didn't seem too happy to be back. She was not the same to us. It was almost like we got on her nerves. Why should she expect all of us to be the same now that she was back? She didn't seem too concerned about hurting all of us or abandoning us. It seemed like all she cared about was herself now…

I know she never came up to me and said, "I am sorry for leaving all of you, Ruthie, and I promise not to ever leave any of you again." That's what we needed was to be reassured by our mother. My God, our lives were turned upside down. I knew we were going to be a little different, but Mom should have known that too.

Ralph was in first grade now and he still didn't understand all of this. But I know one thing that was very good out of all our pain was that we got so close with Daddy and his family. Ralph and Michael went everywhere with Daddy. Uncle Max and Daddy went camping and hunting quite often, and they always took all the boys with them. My brother Hector loved going when he came home on leave. Our love for each other seemed so much stronger than before. I never want that to ever change…

8

That night when we went to bed, I saw Michael sitting on the stairs in the dark. As I walked down the stairs I stopped and I sat next to him and I asked him, "Michael, why are you sitting in the dark?"

Michael looked at me and said, "Ruthie, she is going to leave all of us again."

I then said "Who?"

Michael looked at me and said "Mom." I asked him why he thought that mom was going to leave us again. Michael said that Daddy and Mom were fighting. Then just as he finished his sentence, I heard Daddy telling Mom to tell him the truth, and that she thinks that he is stupid but he knows everything. I started to get scared and I told Michael to go to bed and that everything was going to be all right. Michael just looked at me and said," Ruthie I don't want mom to leave again." I looked at him and said," Michael she won't she will never leave us again I promise you that Mom loves all of us." Michael just smiled and said,"Okay."

Michael went to bed and so did I. As I got ready for bed, I went into the bathroom. I started crying quietly to myself. I then wondered, how long was Michael sitting on the stairs listening and what else did he hear? I thought to myself, *why was Daddy so angry and what was the truth that he needed to know?* Then I remembered all the gossip I kept hearing of my Mom being with Arturo. I knew then, that was the reason Daddy was so angry. After all, Arturo used Daddy and his family and then ran off with his wife and newborn baby.

I didn't know if I was still happy that Mom came back. Our situation seemed to be just as severe as before she came back. It seemed like our pain was still here and she had so much hatred. I couldn't understand why she was so angry. I then started walking up the stairs and I heard my Mom and my Dad talking still.

I froze when I heard my father tell my mother, "I know you just had a baby!" Dad then said to Mom, "You had 11 kids with me. You think I can't tell that you just had a baby?"

Then I could hear my Mom crying, saying, "I don't know what you are talking about."

I was in such shock that I ran up the stairs and jumped into my bed. I started thinking, *Oh my God, if Mom had a baby, that means it's from Arturo, not Daddy.* I thought to myself, *what are we going to do? Everything is getting worse. All of the pain that was supposed to go away now that Mom is back is even stronger and more painful than before. Arturo is Daddy's cousin and if Mom had a baby from him where is the baby? Could Mom had left Arturo and their new baby to come back to Daddy and all of us? I hope she sees that we are her children and her place is with us, not Daddy's cousin!*

From Mom leaving all of us and Daddy, our baby sister was afraid of all of us. All she did was cry whenever we tried to play with her. It was hard for Daddy because she didn't even know him or want Daddy. I know that was hard for Dad, knowing that his own daughter didn't know him. I thought to myself, *Please God, make this nightmare end. My family can't take much more.*

That night was very scary and hard. I didn't get much sleep. Before I could fall asleep, it was time for us to get up for school. Lisa woke us up and I noticed Mom was kind of quiet. I almost asked Mom if everything was all right. But I didn't want her to get mad at Michael and me for listening. I saw that Daddy had already left for work. I tried to put everything out of my mind of what I had over heard. I kept telling myself things had to get better. But as I ate my breakfast, I looked over at Mom and she looked mad. I figured she was mad at Daddy from the argument that I had overheard last night.

All of us were leaving for school and I watched all the little ones kiss Mom good-bye, and for some reason, I didn't see the same loving Mom kiss them back. When I went up to Mom to hug her good-bye, she barely even touched me to hug. It almost felt cold. It was almost like she was a stranger, not the loving Mom that we prayed would come back to all of us. On our way to school, I was thinking how different Mom was now that she came back. I remember how she would really show all of us how much she loved us. And now that she was back, after a whole year, it's like she forgot how to love so many children.

I started wondering if Mom was really with Arturo. I wanted to ask her, but I knew that I couldn't, and if I did, would she get as angry with me as she did with Daddy? Well we got to school, and for some reason, I always pretended everything was fine at home. The nuns were always asking me questions about our well-being. I knew they really just cared, but I hated the fact that everyone knew that our mother left all of us and our father. It was always so embarrassing for me to face.

I would look at all my friends, and their parents were doctors, nurses, teachers, or someone with real responsibility. Here we were with a daddy who worked day and night to keep all of us clothed and in Catholic school. Meanwhile, our Mom leaves all her children for a year and comes back like she never did anything wrong. This was not the picture of a happy family. Now, if all the rumors were true and Mom left with Arturo and had a baby with him, then our lives were even more messed up than I thought.

My first period at school was to go to church. As I walked into church, I made the sign of the cross and kneeled down. I started praying for my family. I prayed for God to make all of this better. I wanted to see Daddy and see if he thought Mom was with Arturo and had a baby with him. I think I would have been able to see it on his face. I think I would have seen the pain and all the betrayal. After I prayed, I felt something run down my leg. I had started bleeding. I got up and ran out of the church. I looked down and it seemed like so much blood. I then ran to the bathroom.

While I was in there, I heard someone walk in. It was Mrs. Jefferies, my social studies teacher. Her son and daughter went to school there as well. Mrs. Jefferies knocked on the door and asked me, "Ruthie, are you all right?"

I answered, "No, I started my period and I don't know what to do. I am so scared!"

Mrs. Jefferies said, "Open the door, Ruthie. I will help you, and you don't need to be afraid. I will show you what to do." I opened the door and she hugged me and said, "Every young girl goes through this." She then asked me if I wanted her to call my mom.

I answered her, "No, I'll be all right." I felt so much better just knowing I was not alone. I looked up and thought to myself, *why don't I want her to call Mom?* Maybe because I really didn't feel like Mom cared like before. That moment I looked at Mrs. Jefferies and wished that she was my mom. She was so loving and warm, just like how my mom used to be.

When we were done, Mrs. Jefferies told me I could stay in the nurse's office until the other kids were ready to go home. I told her that would be great and that I would take my work in the nurse's office with me. I went into the nurse's office and fell asleep on the cot in there.

When school was over, I walked over to get the little ones, to start our walk home. On the way home, I started feeling real sick. Mrs. Jefferies told me that I might start feeling cramps or stomach pains. She also told me to tell my mom, so that she could give me something for pain. I thought to myself that I would tell Mom when I got home. But at the same time, I thought, *why did I not want them to call mom for me?* I guess I was starting to get used to Mom still being gone.

But she was not gone, she was back, and she loves us, so I will tell her when I get home.

When we got home, we walked in and Lisa and Lilly were there. I started to look around for mom but I didn't see her anywhere. I asked Lisa where Mom was and she said, "I think Mom left again, Ruthie."

I looked at Lisa and said, "Oh no she didn't she couldn't leave us again, she just came back!"

Lisa looked at me and I saw a lot of pain in her eyes. Lisa then said, "Well, she did."

I then started to see some anger in Lisa. I thought to myself, *how could Mom leave us again?* I knew that now everything would go back to the point where Lisa did all Moms' work and all of us would go back to the schedule my aunts made for us, just like before.

I asked Lisa, "What are we going to do now?"

Lisa looked over at me and said, "Well, we will do okay without her, just like before."

Lilly then said, "I don't know why she came back in the first place anyway if she was just going to leave us again…"

I could tell Lilly was really mad at Mom. I felt like everyone was. I told Lisa I had started my period today. Lisa looked at me and said, "I'll help you later, Ruthie, okay?"

I said, "Okay."

Everybody was on a roller coaster again, and my starting my period was not really important. I don't even remember feeling any more stomach pains. I guess because my heart was aching so much stronger. I really started feeling very helpless and lost. Everybody looked sad just like before.

Michael came up to me and said, "I want Mom back, Ruthie. I told you she was going to leave again."

We hugged each other, and I thought, *How could she leave again why did she come back in the first place? Every time the little ones are starting to adjust, something happens. Please, God, help my family through all this.*

As I looked up, I saw Daddy had walked inside. Lisa ran up to him and I just saw emptiness in Daddy's face when he hugged Lisa. I knew that Daddy already knew that Mom left again. I somehow felt Mom really didn't want to be our mom again. Maybe it was true—she was with Arturo and she did have another baby. I saw Daddy walk over to the phone to make a call. He was talking in Spanish again, so I knew he was probably talking to one of his brothers or sisters. I walked into Daddy's room and I saw that Mom had taken our little sister Patricia with her. I couldn't understand why she would just keep leaving and taking Patricia, instead of Ralphy or Sandra or even Michael. They were all so little, they still needed their mom. I still needed my mom. All of us still needed our mom!

Daddy hung up the phone, and as he walked into the living room, he told all of us to get ready because we were going to our aunt and uncle's house. Everyone started putting on their shoes and getting their jackets. I looked over at Lisa and she was sitting on the couch hugging Ralphy. I saw my sister for the first time as an adult, not a teenager. She knew exactly how to make all the kids feel better even though she was a kid herself. I felt so sad and angry for my family. I started thinking that I hated her for doing this to all of us! I told myself that I would never forgive her... NEVER!! My family was more torn now than before.

Again it was very close to Christmas, and Mom left again during the same time as last year. I wondered why she always left during the holidays. It always seemed so much harder during Christmas or Thanksgiving. I felt like for the past two years, I started not looking forward to the holiday like I should have, or like I did when I was a kid.

We all went to Aunt Olivia and Uncle Hoss's house for Christmas that year. It was so odd—I started seeing anger instead of pain now on all my family's faces. I knew now I wasn't the only one fed up with Mom's coming and goings. Everyone stayed in the kitchen speaking in Spanish while all the kids played in the other room.

The next few months were very hard. We started hearing more gossip about Mom and Arturo. I started hearing more of Mom having another baby. I even heard it was a girl and they named her after Arturo's mother. I thought to myself, *that's why Mom left again.* But I could not understand why she came back in the first place!! I know it was a lot less work with just two kids than with all of us. But we were her children too. Her place was with all of us, being a mother. I told myself I would never be like my mom. She showed no loyalty to Daddy or his family. How could this heartless action be good? She would feel as much pain someday as we did right then. Arturo will ask someday, how could a good mother or wife do this to her family? He will not see true happiness either because he is a dog for doing this to HIS own family. There is no way they can find true happiness.

We were accepting the fact that Mom was with Arturo. We really never showed each other how we felt. I never would bring up Mom to my other siblings. I just didn't want to feel like I wanted her home or that I missed her. If they missed her, I didn't want to remind them of their pain. I could tell that Michael and Sandra and even Ralphy missed her. Even after she spanked Ralphy, I could tell that he missed her tremendously.

A few months passed by and Lisa had a sweet sixteen party. She had a huge cake and music and everything. I remember that Daddy wore sunglasses. At first, I really didn't understand why, but now I know he was trying to hide his pain. Everyone helped out in planning the big party for Lisa. All of our aunts and uncles helped Daddy. I know all of my family were very proud of Lisa for all the help she gives to us and to our father. They wanted to do this for her and make it Lisa's special day. Lisa looked like a real princess. I could tell that Daddy really tried to make our lives as normal as he could, but I could tell it was hard for him to see all of us and think, how could the mother of his kids do this to them? As time went on all of us seemed to adjust with not having a mother. I tried my best to not think about my mom or her actions. I knew I needed to just keep going and to not dwell on all of this. I think even if I didn't bring mom up, daddy always seem to think about her and what she did to his children.

I remember I had wanted to run for queen in a school fundraiser. Each ticket cost one dollar and each ticket counted as one vote. On the day of the fundraiser, our school was like a big carnival. We had so many different booths and games. We even had booths with things to buy. Daddy gave all of us money that morning for us to use at the fundraiser. I had collected around 75 dollars from our neighbors and family for the queen contest.

Then, as we were at a booth trying to win a prize, Michael said, "Ruthie, there is Daddy." I looked up and saw Daddy all dressed up. He always looked so handsome in his suits. Before I knew it I was running towards him. Then as I ran to him, I said," daddy look I have 75 votes for the contest.". "Do you think I might win daddy?"

Daddy looked at me and said, "You have a lot more than that." Daddy then gave me a bag. When I looked in the bag, I saw so many ones and five-dollar bills. I asked Daddy what all the money was for. He looked at me and said, "It's for your contest for queen. All the men from my work wanted to buy tickets from you."

I was so excited. I hugged Daddy and said, "Thank you, Daddy! Tell everyone at your work thank you for me, okay?" I then ran to give all the money to Sister Maryanne. Sister Maryanne looked at me and said, "Oh my goodness, Ruthie, this is quite a few votes." She then started counting all the money. Sister Maryanne looked at me and said, "Ruthie, tell your father thank you from all of us."

I said okay and then ran back to find Daddy and tell him what Sister Maryanne said. I saw Daddy talking to his friends and I told him the school said thank you for all the votes. I then ran to see where Ralph and Sandra were. Then I saw them trying to win goldfish with Michael. Before I knew it, they won like five goldfish. Daddy said we could keep them, and the little ones were pretty excited about that.

When it came time for the announcement for queen, I was so nervous. Most of our aunts and uncles were there. All of them belonged to the same church. A lot of my cousins went to our school also. So it was nice being there with all the family. Everyone was there except Mom. Sister Maryanne started reading the number of votes everyone received who had entered. When she called my name as the winner, I was so excited; I started running up the driveway to where her booth was. Sister Maryanne leaned down and hugged me. She then placed a crown on my head that the school had made for me. I felt so happy that day I didn't want the day to end. I really felt like a normal kid that day.

Everyone was clapping, all my friends and all my family. It was such a good feeling; the only thing missing to make everything perfect was our mother. After I won, I started feeling sad because a boy named Ricky in my class was saying the only reason I won was because my daddy bought all the tickets himself. I was embarrassed and hurt by what he said. I just wanted to turn around and punch him.

Then I started thinking, *did Daddy do that? And if he did, it's only because he loves me so much.* After the celebration was over, we went home and I tried not to think about what stupid Ricky said. I thought, *He is always a bad kid. Why should I listen to anything he says?* But then I thought maybe Daddy wanted me to win so that I would not think about all the bad things going on in our lives. I loved that day I thought that it was such a perfect day for all of us. The little ones won a bunch of toys and fish and I won for queen so it was a great day.

9

A few weeks went by, and one day when we were playing out in the front of our home, I saw the postman come to our home. He stopped right in front of our house. The postman stepped out of his car and walked around to reach for something. Then he got out a huge box. He then lifted up the box and as he started walking up the sidewalk, I remember asking him, "Who is that box for?"

The postman looked at all of us and said, "It's for all of you kids." All of us just looked at each other and smiled. We all were so excited; we had never received a big box in the mail before. It wasn't anyone's birthday or anything like that. So we were pretty excited to see that this huge box was for us. We tried to run inside with the box. It was too heavy, so the postman told us to let him set it down for us. Michael opened the front door to our house and the postman sat the huge box on our sofa. The postman smiled at all of us and said," enjoy kids." We then looked over to him and said," Thank you Mr. Postman." We then yelled for Lisa to come and see what we got.

When Lisa came out from the other room, she said, "Hey, who is that big box from?" We then looked for the label that had the name on it, and it said "Mom." All of us just looked at each other and before we knew it we had started to open up the box. We were trying very hard to get the tape apart so that we could see what was inside. The little ones were very excited to get such a big gift in the mail. It was so neat seeing them so happy. But I could tell Lisa wasn't as happy for all of us. She probably knew that this was another example of Mom playing with our feelings.

The box was finally opened. Inside were many gifts for all of us. There were stuffed bears, baseball caps, T-shirts, puzzles, coloring books, baseball mitts, and more. Everything in the box was labeled from the Chicago zoo, the Chicago Cubs, and the Chicago Bears. I guessed that was where Mom was, in Chicago. I then looked at Lisa and said, "Lisa, there is no letter in the box." Lisa didn't say anything. I then told her, "I guess Mom is in Chicago."

Lisa said, "Yeah, I guess she is." Lisa seemed like she had a lot on her mind. I could tell she was really thinking of a lot of different things at once. Meanwhile, all the little kids were running around the house with all the things Mom sent, and we were pretty excited too. I was so happy to get a gift from Mom even though it was not anyone's birthday. It was nice just knowing that Mom was thinking about us and that she loved us enough to send all of us such a large gift. I just couldn't understand why Mom didn't send us a letter.

Before we knew it, Daddy walked in. All the kids were running around him with the T-shirts on. The boys were wearing the baseball caps and had toys in their hands. Sandra had a bear in her arms and so did I. Lisa and Lilly have gifts too. There were so many things in the box, we didn't know what to grab first.

Then Daddy looked at us and said, "Where did ya'll get all these things?"

We ran up to him all at once and said, "Mom sent them to us. The postman brought them."

Daddy then walked over to the kitchen and picked up the box. He turned around and asked all of us to put everything back in the box. He said, "Let me see all the things your mom sent. Put them all in the box so that I can see it all."

We looked at each other but didn't really think too much about it. All of us started taking off our hats and shirts and gathering up all the stuffed bears. The boys even had baseball mitts that said Chicago Cubs on them. We put everything back in the box and Daddy closed the box and walked outside. All of us just looked at each other. Daddy didn't say a word. All of us followed him, and watched him place the box on the barbeque pit. He then put lighter fluid all over the huge box. As I watched, and before I could scream, "Stop!" Daddy lit a match and burned everything. All the little ones started screaming for Daddy to stop. Daddy kept putting more and more lighter fluid on the box. Meanwhile it seemed like the fire kept getting bigger and bigger.

Everyone was screaming and crying. I looked over at Lisa and I saw her covering Ralphy and Sandra's eyes. Lilly was hugging Michael. I then ran and grabbed the back of Daddy's shirt. As I pulled his shirt, I begged him to stop. But Daddy just kept adding more lighter fluid to the fire. All of us were so devastated. I was devastated; I couldn't imagine the pain my little brothers and sister were feeling. I knew that I felt like dying that day. I looked over at the barbeque pit and the box was a huge pile of ashes. After the box burned, Daddy just walked past all of us and walked inside the house. I saw him crying when he walked past me. I was crying too. All of us were crying; the little ones seemed like they would cry forever. Their cry seemed so loud; my heart ached for each of them and for myself.

As we all looked over at the burned box, we felt so helpless and sad. I know Daddy didn't want to hurt any of us. I know that now. But looking at Sandra, Michael, and Ralphy's faces that night, I didn't have the words to explain to them that Daddy just loves all of us so much that he doesn't want Mom hurting us by coming in and out of our lives. I think Daddy thought that Mom couldn't fix her mistake by sending us this huge box of gifts so many months after leaving us not once but twice! When all of us went into the house, Daddy said, "You don't need anything from your mother! Even a dog doesn't leave her puppies." We were so upset and I felt so sorry for the little ones because they were too little to understand why Daddy felt that way. I think I was too little to understand any of this myself.

Lisa then told all of us to go inside. We sat in the living room, devastated. I looked over at the little ones, who were crying still. They were not even watching television. Lisa kept hugging every one of us and I was feeling so grateful for having such a compassionate sister. It felt good to be loved and hugged by my sister.

A short while later, Daddy walked out from his room and said, "All of you get in the car. We are going somewhere." All of us looked at each other and did as we were told. I saw a confused look on Lisa's face. Lisa had been sitting on the couch trying to calm Sandra and Ralphy down. Lilly, Michael, and I were just crying and looking at each other. We all got up and walked outside, and then we got into the car. Daddy didn't say a word. As I looked out the window I noticed Daddy was driving us to Kmart. I looked over at the little ones and they were trying their best to stop crying. Daddy had Ralphy and Sandra's hands, and Lisa had Michael's hand; Lilly and I just followed as we all walked into Kmart. We were so excited; we loved going shopping and we really didn't go shopping anymore now that Mom left.

When we got inside Kmart, we were following Daddy. He walked over to the toys and said "Pick you out something, okay? All of you can get something."

The little ones had stopped crying; now they were very excited. I saw Daddy smile with watery eyes. Dad was just watching the little ones pick out a toy. All of us picked out something and daddy paid for all of it at the register. The little ones seemed to be doing better now that they knew their daddy was not mad at them. I think they were just confused. I know I was very confused at first also. The drive home was quiet, but the little ones seemed like they were having a good time with their new toys. That night, I knew my father did what he thought was right. We were so happy that night after going to Kmart with daddy... Sometimes I think we forgot all about the big box that came in the mail that day. But now, as a grown woman, I can still picture the pain in all the faces of everyone that I love. I don't think I will ever forget the look on my little brothers' and my little sister's faces. I know I will never forget their pain for the rest of my life.

I then started thinking that Daddy must have felt bad for burning all of our things from Mom. But then I know he started feeling angry. I know dad probably thought, why would Mom think she can leave all of us twice within a year and still be able to send us gifts and receive our love? Then I started getting really angry and I thought to myself, *Even a dog don't leave her puppies.*

Time went on and all of us were adjusting the best we could. Daddy still worked a lot so we hardly ever saw him. I remember we would write him notes and leave them on the kitchen table for him to read when he came home. I would write him a note for school supplies or "girl stuff" for my period. This was so much easier for Daddy. He would leave us money on top of the note to let us know he read it. He never said no; he always gave to all of us whenever we needed it.

I remember I was embarrassed to ask him for money for sanitary napkins or for bras and underwear. Lisa told me not to be embarrassed. Daddy knew what young girls go through. We seemed to be writing notes for everything. Underclothes, school supplies, and lunch money. That was okay; sometimes I kind of liked writing those notes because at the end of the note, I wrote "Love you, Daddy. Your daughter, Ruthie."

Gosh, I love my daddy so much. He is everything a daddy is supposed to be. One thing was for sure: Daddy would never leave us.

10

Well, a few years went by, and still we hardly heard a peep out of Mom. I started hating Mom for not caring about any of us and for not coming home to take care of all of us. Mom started calling once in awhile. I think everyone forgave her for leaving. I am not sure. We really never talked about mom to each other. I could not get myself to talk on the phone to her without feeling angry at her for destroying my childhood. I seen the girls talk on the phone to her and I always act like I had something to do just to avoid her. I remember one day Lisa and I were walking to the beach and I noticed her belly was a little bigger than normal. I then asked her why she was gaining weight. Lisa looked at me and started crying, then said, "I think I am pregnant."

I am sure Lisa was scared, and I was afraid for her too. I don't know how Lisa told daddy but before I knew it daddy knew. I don't think Daddy liked the idea very much, but I know it was because he wanted Lisa to enjoy her life, since she had been so devoted to all of us for the last few years. Lisa was acting mother and sister to all of us.

71

That January, Lisa had a boy and she named him Jesse. Gosh, Jesse was a handsome baby. I loved watching him for Lisa. I knew Lisa would never take Jesse from us the way Mom took our sister. My dad adored Jesse. Daddy really helped Lisa a lot with Jesse. I always thought that was so good of Daddy to help my sister. Jesse's father died when he was a few years old. He was a little older than Lisa, so I think that's why Daddy was always so concerned for her and her baby boy.

A little later, our father adopted Jesse so that he would be fully covered under his insurance if anything should happen to him. I always thought that was pretty cool of Daddy to do for Lisa and her baby. All the girls started having kids and started getting married. Lisa and I both got married. Shortly after I got married, I realized that getting married was a bad idea. I was not happy at all. But I felt that getting married meant one less kid for my dad to worry about.

I was working after school at the Unemployment Office. I really liked it. I felt that someday I would be a boss just like my father. I tried my best not to need my mother for anything. It seemed like every time one of my sisters had a baby; Mom would come into our lives again.

Mom never came to Galveston for me, but she came for Lisa, Lilly, and Sandra. That was okay with me. Mom stayed with them through their deliveries, then six weeks later. I wanted that for them since my sisters seemed to like having Mom in their lives again. It seemed they needed her more than I did anyway.

Daddy used to tell me I was the strongest out of the girls. I wasn't too sure about that because Lisa survived all the load of raising all of us when she was barely in high school. But somehow, I felt proud when my father would tell me that. I always felt kind of special when I heard from my father that I was strong. That always meant the world to me; I guess because I knew how strong he was for all of us.

Years went by, and after having three children, my husband was getting more and more abusive to me. I hated being married. I wasn't used to a man treating me so badly since my father and my brothers never even shoved me or hit me. So I decided that the best thing for me and my children was to leave my abusive husband. One night, while I was babysitting my nephew Wick and my three children, my husband walked out of the bathroom. He started acting really mean and he was banging on the table, scaring the kids. At that point I knew I needed to leave him and I needed to leave him NOW!

I started cleaning the bathroom and I saw a spoon on the floor. It must have fallen out of the pocket of his pants. I then went into the bedroom, and he was acting so out of control that I started packing all my things to leave him. I called his father to come get him so that I could leave. When he seen me on the phone he started hitting me. I was trying so hard to get away from him, but he was so strong he would not even budge. My kids were screaming their heads off and my nephew was terrified. I kept trying to get away from his grip. I was so scared I thought he was going to kill me. Before I knew it I heard his father say," What the hell is going on?" Then his father grabbed him and they started fist fighting. I was so terrified I didn't know what to do next. I ran to the phone, and before I knew it, I had called my mom. I asked her for help and asked her if I could go to her home for a while. Mom told me yes, and she said she would send someone to pick me and the kids up. At the time, my mom had moved from Chicago to California.

Her best friend's husband Benny came to pick me up. The kids and I stayed at their home until I flew to California the next day. I called my sister-in-law to pick up my nephew from Benny and Mary's house. The next day, I was wondering what made me call Mom and not Dad. I thought that Mom knew how to run and hide without being found. Dad probably would have wanted me to try to work out my marriage. My boy's names are David and Daniel and my daughter's name is Sondra. David looked really scared and Daniel and Sondra would not let go of me. I tried my best to calm them down but I knew I needed to run away. They were so afraid when they seen their father so violent with their mother and their grandfather. I was trying my best to hurry. I knew I needed to save my own life. That night I looked in the mirror at Mary's house and I had a busted lip and a black eye. I told myself that day I would never go back to him, NEVER.

I started thinking, *why did my husband have a spoon in his pocket?* Then I knew that he must have been doing drugs. I knew I was doing the best thing for me and my kids. I really don't know what I was thinking, to go and stay at Mom's house—the same house she shared with Arturo and their baby and with my dad's daughter. But I needed to get out of my marriage and get out of Texas.

Mom helped me out by watching my daughter Sondra and picking up David and Daniel from school for me… I enrolled at a beauty school two weeks after I arrived in California. I had met some great friends there. On my first day of beauty school I was sitting outside with all of the new students. Everyone there seemed to know someone, and then this girl asked me what my name was I looked at her and said,"Ruthie what is yours?" She looked at me and said her name was Jenny. We started talking and we got along very well. I knew we would be friends for a very long time. I am so close with Jenny even almost twenty years later. I missed my family very much. But I found myself getting very close with Jenny's family. That really helped me and the kids. It seemed like they were very close to each other just like my family is to each other.

Mom was already married to our cousin Arturo. They did have a daughter and they did name her Esther after his mom. I kind of thought all of what she did was unforgivable, but I thought to myself, *I really need to try for all of our sakes.* All of my brothers and sisters seemed to accept any kind of relationship with mom that they could get. Daddy seemed like he forgave her. He never talked bad about her or anything like that. My sisters seemed to love having her in their lives again.

I guess I still had a lot of resentment in my heart for all the pain that I saw my entire family endure. But I kept telling myself I was really going to try to have a real relationship with my mother. I was going to try to not think about all the years she wasn't there. I was going to think that right now she was here for me when I really needed her to be One day when I was at school; I had seen that the daughter of a friend of my mother and Arturo's came into the beauty school for me to do her hair. She had wanted a permanent so I knew she was going to be at the school awhile. So while I was giving her a permanent, we started talking. She told me that my mom didn't look old enough to have a daughter as old as me, and three grandchildren. I responded by saying that I was the sixth child of my mother and father. She then told me that my mom told her mom and dad that she was married to my father and had me, and then she married Arturo and had my two younger sisters. I stopped what I was doing. I then looked at her in her eyes. When I looked into her eyes I knew she was telling the truth.

I really started to get angry. I decided to set the record straight by telling her that my mom was married to my father for many many years and that they had 11 children together, and that my oldest brother died when he was a baby. I then told her that among the living, there are ten children from my mother and father and one from my mother and Arturo. I also stated that my mother and father had many grandchildren together. Also that mine were in the middle, they were not the oldest or the youngest out of all the grandchildren.

This girl looked pretty shocked; she told me that her mother told her all the facts that she had just told me. I looked at her and said, "Well, that's what your mother thinks, but when I see your mom, I will tell her the truth." I also said, "Well, I am not my mother's only child from my father, and you will see, because my second-oldest brother is coming to visit me soon." I also told her that I know that she had met my uncle Memo, a.k.a. William, when he came to visit my mother and that my second-oldest brother is William, named after my uncle Memo.

Then she kind of gave me a weird look. But somehow I knew that she realized I was telling the truth. I was so angry; why did Mom say all those lies to these good people? The whole thing didn't make any sense. I guess it would be kind of hard to tell people that you took off with your husband's cousin and left all but one of ten children behind with your husband.

I knew then that she didn't know that Arturo was family to my dad and to me. Then I started thinking maybe Mom didn't want them to know that, or that she was a lot older than Arturo. I didn't care and if she would have continued talking about it, I sure would have told her more to set my family's record straight. But I dropped the topic and figured she would go home and tell her parents what

I told her about my family. I finished her hair and somehow we stopped talking about Mom's lies.

But for the rest of the day, I couldn't stop thinking of how my mother could deny having all of her own kids. I thought she was pretty good friends with these people. Whatever reason Mom had for lying about having all of us as her children was enough reason for her to be here and live a so-called happy life. *How could she do all this,* I kept thinking to myself. Maybe she was hoping none of us would ever come and visit her here with Arturo.

Then suddenly I thought to myself that they really didn't even know Mom's real age. So it seemed accurate that I was her oldest child. But still I felt angry and hurt that she would deny having all of us. That day, after school, I had laid the kids down for bed. Then suddenly I remembered that it was Daddy's birthday. I thought to myself, *Great, I hope Daddy doesn't pick up on my anger and the hurt I feel for Mom right now.*

I went to the phone to call Daddy, and after speaking to him, I wanted so much to tell him what I had found out. But then I thought about it and I didn't want to worry my father or make him angry at Mom for hurting his children again. After I spoke with my father and told him happy birthday, I called my younger sister Patricia to the phone and told her to wish our father a happy birthday.

I recall my sister Esther was snickering and giggling on her bed. I looked at her and asked her what her problem was. She just kept on laughing. Then I asked her what was so damn funny. For a minute there, I thought that somehow maybe Mom already knew what I found out and that she told Esther. Esther had always been so damn nosey. Every time I looked at her, I would think to myself, *you are a product of your mother and father screwing around behind my father's back!*

I tried to stop myself from getting off track. I needed to find out what the heck was so damn funny to this sister/cousin of mine. Finally she answered in between her laughs and said, "Oh, I didn't know today was your dad's birthday."

I looked at her and said, "So what, why is that so damn funny?"

Esther then looked at me and she started laughing even harder, saying, "Well, today is your dad's birthday and today is my mom and dad's anniversary!" She just kept on laughing, saying, "Isn't that funny?"

I was so mad, I just looked at her and told her, "You better shut up or I will shut you up myself." Then I started walking towards the kitchen. In the kitchen, I saw Mom washing the dishes. She had just finished with dinner, and Arturo was in the shower. My kids were watching television in the living room. I sat down on the chair in the kitchen. Then I looked at her, and she looked so happy and content. But before I could think of what to say, I had already started to ask her question after question.

I started by saying to her, "Mom is this true that today is your anniversary?" She looked at me and said yes. I stared at her and said, "Oh, so it wasn't enough to hurt Daddy by leaving him and all of his kids for his cousin, but you two dirty asses went and got married on his birthday? Well Mom, you really kept that secret good, almost as good as your whereabouts when you left me and all my brothers and sisters."

Mom just looked at me and started crying. I didn't care if I was hurting her or not. All I kept thinking was this was not a coincidence that they married on Daddy's birthday nor was it a coincidence that they ended up together with a daughter. Neither one of them had any respect for their family or themselves. I wanted my mom to tell me how she left all of us and why. I knew no one had asked her before. I guess they were afraid she might walk out of their lives again. But I felt that I needed to know the whole truth of why she left all of us. I needed to know from her mouth to my ears why she left us for Arturo. And where did they go when they left my dad's house?

I told her that every time she left, Lisa had to do everything for all of us. I told her that our sister was also a mother for many years to all of us. I also said that she took Lisa's childhood away from her. Lisa was only in high school at the time our mother decided to leave all her children for her husband's cousin. My poor sister didn't deserve to be given all that responsibility. She didn't deserve to lose so much just for our mother's actions.

I told Mom, "Lisa did your job for so many years." I also said "Ralphy looks at Lisa as his mother. Lisa was both mother and sister to all of us. Don't you feel the least bit guilty for doing all this to all of your children?" I then started telling Mom everything that I knew. I told her about the girl who came into the salon that day. I told her how she thought that I was Mom's oldest daughter. I looked at her and said, "How can you sleep at night? How can you deny your own flesh and blood?"

Mom looked at me and started telling me that she tried to go back to all of us. But my daddy kept telling her horrible things. I looked at her and said, "Can you blame him? Arturo was his damn cousin and he lived with all of us!" I then said, "Mom, he is Daddy's family!!"

Mom started telling me that Arturo showed her attention and she was lonely because Daddy worked so much. I remember telling her that Daddy worked long hours for us and for HER! I asked her who helped her leave and how did she leave? Mom then started telling me that my grandmother Ruth helped her and Arturo get away.

I couldn't believe what I heard, but then I always had a feeling that my grandmother Ruth knew where Mom was. I guess I was trying to give her the benefit of the doubt. I started thinking all that time it was all fake; she knew exactly where our mom was and who she was with. I thought to myself, *my grandmother is dirty just like Mom.* It was the same amount of betrayal as my mother leaving us, versus my grandmother knowing where she was all of that time. And helping her get there.

Gosh, I couldn't believe it; Grandma helped Mom leave all of her own children. I was sitting there in a state of shock. How a grandmother could hurt so many little kids and how could a mother hurt so many of her own flesh and blood? I told her, "Dad knew Grandma Ruth knew where you were the whole time." I told her that they thought my father was stupid, but he wasn't; he knew everything. Mom started telling me that Daddy wasn't as innocent as I thought. She said Dad hired a private investigator to find them. Then, when the private investigator found them in Chicago, Dad called the Immigration Department to report Arturo as an illegal alien. That was probably why they moved to California.

Mom said that the Immigration Department deported Arturo back to Mexico while she was still pregnant with Esther. I told her, "Again, Mom, do you blame Dad for his actions?"

Then, before I knew it, Arturo came out of the shower. He looked at me and he looked at Mom. I guess he could tell that my mom was upset with the conversation. He started telling me to leave my mom alone and that I was to respect his home. I looked at him and said, "Yeah, OKAY, I will respect your home, just like you respected my father's home when you lived with us. And then you ran off with his wife, you coward!" I then told him that he was a coward because he ran and hid himself from my father. I told him he was lucky that he ran from Texas because he probably would have been dead if my brothers had found out what he was doing to all of us and to their father.

Then he started yelling at me in Spanish. I remember him saying that Mom being with him was my father's own fault. He said that my daddy never showed my mom love or attention. He then said if Daddy was good to Mom, she would never have left him. He said that my mom had left him after she had Esther, and went back to my father to try to work things out. He then said Daddy treated Mom like shit, so she left him and us again.

I was so mad, I started yelling at him. I started telling him that he was Daddy's cousin and he should be ashamed of himself doing this to his own family. I told him, "The only reason Mom came back to Daddy was to take money from him."

Arturo looked at me and said, "We don't need anything from your father."

I told him, "Bullshit! That's why Mom stole all that money from him when she came back."

Arturo looked at me and said, "That money was your mom's money that was in the bank in her name only.

I asked him, "Where in the hell do you think that money came from? My father, that's where. My mom NEVER worked a day in her life while she was married to my dad!" I also told him that I knew my father sent Mom money for herself and my sister. I then said, "Hell, my father even sent Mom money for your wetback daughter!" I told him, "That's how all of you pay your bills, with my father's money." I told them they were both dirt and what comes around goes around. I looked at my mother and said, "You will never have what you had with my dad!" Then I looked at Arturo and said, "You will get what you have coming to you, my mom will leave you too, just like she left her own kids and family." I told him, "You will never be as great as a man as my father is. You are a wetback and you will always be a wetback."

I ran to the room and got all my things together. I then woke up my kids. As I was getting them ready to leave, I was thinking, *where in the name of God am I going to go?* Then Arturo came into the room and told me he wanted me out of his house. I told him I didn't want to be in his house anyway, and that there was bad karma there. I also told him it was evil there; they were evil, him and my mom.

I then started to walk to my friend's house. When I walked out of the house, Arturo and my mom both told me never to come back. I said, "Fine. I should have never come to your unholy, filthy house in the first place."

At that time, I didn't know what I was going to do, so far away from my real home. One of my friends was married and she only lived a few blocks from Mom and one block from my son's school. I was so upset, I couldn't think. I didn't know what to do next. Here I was in California, so far from my family in Texas. I don't know what the heck I was thinking when I came here. My oldest son, David, kept asking me if I was all right. I told him yes. Then he asked me "Mom, where are we going to sleep tonight?" I tried my best to reassure him that everything would work itself out. Then I told him that we would be fine. But deep down inside, I wasn't sure if we would be all right.

I started praying for guidance from God. I really started missing home now that I was here, so far away from the people who meant so much to me. I started remembering that all of my mother's friends thought that I was the oldest of my mother's kids. Mom never told anyone about all of us. Mom told everyone I was from my dad and the two girls were from Arturo. I let them all know that I had many brothers and sisters, all of us children from Mom and Dad! Then I realized she had been living this lie for so long. I don't think Mom even thought that it was wrong not to claim all of us as her children.

Well, I got to one of my friend's home her name is Cheryl. Cheryl said I was more than welcome to stay with them. I stayed up that night with my friend. I just cried and cried. I told her that everything I had heard was accurate. I told her about when Michael and I sat on the stairs listening to Mom and Dad fight about her having a baby. I told her that Mom had been pretending that she only had three girls, and that I was the only one from my dad.

Cheryl just looked at me. I don't think she ever heard such painful and heart-wrenching incidents as the ones I just told her. She told me everything would be all right and that I could stay there with her. I was grateful but I knew I needed to find my own place with my children. I knew I couldn't take my kids back to Texas; I needed to stay away from my abusive husband.

11

Time went by and all that was okay with me. I was already used to not having a mother, but my children were not used to not having a grandmother. They really loved her and sometimes I think she really loved them. I remember seeing a look on Mom's face like she hated me. I guess that's true because I hated all the hurt she had caused all of us. I survived being in California away from Mom. I rented my own place for me and the kids. It was a three-bedroom townhouse and I really enjoyed living alone with just my kids. I finished beauty school and started working for me and the kids. At the time, I was a photographer. I was making very good money and I was happy.

I went to Texas as often as I could. I still was not talking to Mom. I knew the best thing for her and I was to stay away from each other. I had some really good friends in California. One of them was named Kathy. Kathy had a very loving mother and many sisters. Gosh, I was so close with all of them. They reminded me of my close family. They adored each other and they loved their mother so much. I loved watching them as a family.

One of my really close friends was named Bebe. I met Bebe at the beauty school I attended with Jenny. I loved her and her family very much. Many times, I thanked God for blessing me with such great friends. I think they had a lot to do with my strength in dealing with all of my mother's actions. Many times when I felt homesick, I would go and spend time with my girlfriends and their families, and I always felt like I was back home with my loving family in Texas.

A few months later, the kids and I went to church. While I was in church, I saw another family of friends of my mother and Arturo. The woman came up to me and said hi and asked me how I had been. After talking awhile, the daughter told me that she had met my sister Sandra. She then started saying that Sandra must look just like her mother because she doesn't look anything like me. I just looked at her. Then it dawned on me that they think Sandra is my sister but not my mother's daughter. Again I had to set the record straight and I started to tell her that Sandra and I have the same parents. I proceeded to tell her what happened to all of us when we were just kids. I also told her that she wasn't the first person my mom lied to about having so many kids.

I started to tell her about the other incident that happened to me before my mom kicked me out of her home. This woman started apologizing to me for bringing up such painful memories. She also told me that whatever reason my mother has for denying her children, only God will be her judge. She told me that it must have been pretty hard for my mother to leave all of us and her family. I started getting really angry and told her I didn't think it was too hard for my mother because she came back to us and left us again within a week. But that time, she didn't even leave a note or anything like that.

I know this woman was shocked, but at the same time, I know she knew that she could never really trust my mother or anything that she says. After that, my mother stopped talking to her as well as the other family of friends. I guess she was embarrassed for everything that she did, and now that I was here, everyone knew what she did so many years ago.

A year or so later, I found out my husband was in a severe auto accident. He suffered severe brain injury and died two days later. I felt bad for my children but I also felt that now I could truly start my life over again. I always lived with the fear that he would come one night and take my kids from me. I thought to myself, *I don't ever have to be afraid again.*

We went down for the funeral and I don't think my kids really understood what death was. My father paid for most of the funeral and I knew it was because of my children. Again, I always thought my father was the greatest man there was. I tried to go home to Texas as often as I could. Daddy loved it when we came home. He took David and Daniel camping every time we were in town. Uncle Max always went camping with them. The boys loved their uncle and their grandpa. I felt that Dad and Uncle Max were trying their best to be a father figure to my boys now that their dad had died.

A few years went by, and I remarried. I had two children with my new husband, a boy named Richard and a girl named Alicia. Now I have five children. My new husband was pretty strict with my boys and my daughter from my late husband. Sometimes I felt like he just did not like them. I tried not to think negatively, but as time went by, he started getting worse. Whenever I was at work, he was really mean to them. David was involved in track at school, and Daniel was involved in baseball. I felt the less time they were around him, the better.

Then, in 1990, my father started getting sick quite often. Daddy had diabetes and he drank alcohol, so that really didn't help at all. Soon after, Dad was forced to medically retire. I really think that was devastating for him. He was so used to working and being in charge. Not working put him somewhat in a state of depression. A little later, Lisa told me that my brothers were building a room for Daddy at her house so that she could take care of him. I knew Daddy was in great hands with Lisa as his caretaker.

I thought to myself, *I will always be grateful to my sister for taking care of all of us and now our father.* Lisa never seemed to hesitate when it came to her family. During this time, Lisa was happily married. My brother-in-law was just as great as my sister. Together they had three additional children, along with my nephew Jesse. I was really thankful to God for giving my sister such a great life. But now Lisa was to start caring for Dad. I knew that she didn't mind. Lisa adored Daddy, and Daddy adored Lisa. But at the same time, I wished I lived back in Texas to take care of my father myself.

Dad moved in with Lisa and my brother-in-law. Lisa took very good care of Daddy just like she took good care of all of us. Daddy soon had to be on dialysis for his diabetes. That was a strain on Daddy and on Lisa. Daddy had to go to dialysis two, sometimes three times a week. The doctor's office was about 20 minutes from Lisa's house. Plus, he was on many different medications. Lisa was very good at caring for Dad. It seemed like that is her calling is to be a caregiver. Lisa was very good at giving dad the medication when he needed it and with or without food. I will forever be in her debt for everything she has done for all of us and now for our father.

Time went on and I called Daddy every Sunday to see how he was doing. Dad would tell me he was doing fine and it always seemed like he was doing just fine. But then Lisa had told me different things that were going wrong with Dad's health.

In January of 1991, Lisa called me and told me Daddy was in the hospital. I then decided I needed to be home with Dad and my family. I asked my husband if I could go home to spend time with my father and to help my sister with him. He agreed, as long as I took the kids with me. So I made arrangements to go home with all five of my children.

When we got to the airport, the kids were getting really excited to see their family. The kids and I sat down on the plane, waiting for it to take off. As the plane took off, my youngest daughter got her arm stuck in between the seats, and it broke her arm. She cried the whole flight to Texas. The airline had a medic waiting for us to have her checked out by a doctor.

After the doctor's office fixed her up, we headed for the hospital to see Dad. When I walked into his room, he looked so frail it scared me. Daddy had a red light taped on the tip of his finger. It was a monitor of some sort, and he pointed it at the babies. The little ones thought he had a light on his finger just like E.T.

Dad kept pointing his finger at the little ones. They laughed at Dad and I could tell they were getting comfortable with their grandpa. Dad was hooked up to so many monitors it really frightened me. After an hour or so went by, Daddy got out of his bed to go to the bathroom. I started helping him and I started crying when I saw how slow he was walking.

The doctor said Daddy had a pacemaker put in him to regulate his heart. If Daddy's heart went too fast, then the pacemaker would slow it down. But if his heart beat too slow, then the pacemaker would help it get up to speed. That really scared me, because I didn't remember Daddy really ever being sick. If he ever was, he was too busy and had too many kids for him to ever complain.

Later that year, I flew home four times to be with Daddy and my family. During one of the visits with my father, I stayed at Lisa's house. I knew she needed a rest from caring for Daddy. I had suggested that they go out of town and get some rest, and that I would care for Daddy. I watched the kids for my sister, and Michael's kids as well. My sister and brother and their spouses left me in charge of their children and our father.

I remember my niece Melanie, Lisa's daughter, was being really bad. I walked into the room and told her to go kneel down in the bathroom until she learned to behave. She was pretty upset with me but she did it. Melanie then started crying, because in the bathroom I had put rice on the floor for her to kneel on. I remember my dad walked by the bathroom where she was kneeling and he started laughing and pointing at her. I looked around the corner and saw Dad. Melanie started crying even more; she was so mad at her grandpa for making fun of her.

I asked my dad to stop and he just laughed and said, "She's a mean mother."

I laughed, but at the same time I knew my niece would learn her lesson with her aunt Ruthie. That weekend, I saw firsthand how hard it was to care for my father along with a husband and children. Again it seemed like my sister did it without complaining.

It seemed like every two to three months, Daddy kept getting worse. The doctors kept telling all of us that Dad's condition didn't look good. In May of 1991 my little Sister Sandra was planning to get married. I was very happy for my little sister. But I was so upset that I was not able to see my little Sister get married. My husband had told me I had gone to Texas too many times that year. He said it had cost us quite a bit of money, me flying back and forth from California to Texas.. I knew that daddy really needed me there and I needed to be there. I agreed that I would not attend Sandra's wedding. I called Texas and spoke to Sandra and explained my situation to her. Sandra said she was sorry I could not go to her wedding but that she understood that I needed to stay home. I spoke with everyone after the wedding to see how everything went; my family told me that Daddy walked Sandra down the aisle to marry my new Brother in law David. I was so happy for Sandra I knew that was very exciting for her. Daddy was so sick that year it was amazing he was able to walk at all. . My sister Lisa told me he had a hard time walking down the aisle but he did it for his baby girl. I started crying because I knew that that meant the world to our father, to give his daughter away. I know that Daddy has always been very proud of Sandra and he would not have missed walking her down the aisle no matter what. I was so happy that my daddy made Sandra's day a perfect one. In June daddy started getting worse. My sister in law Jodie called me and told me my daddy was in the hospital again. I then asked to speak to my brother Hector or Willie. Hector got on the phone and told me that daddy was getting worse. Hector also said that I needed to come home to be with daddy. Hector said," Ruthie it doesn't look good." I told Hector I will call with the information on my flight back home. I spoke to my husband. I told him that my family said that my father was getting worse. My husband hesitated but agreed for me to go home but again with all of my children. I made my reservations back and I was at the hospital within 18 hours from that phone call. Daddy had got very bad. We thought we were going to lose him several times. I ended up staying in Texas for a whole month. I didn't want to leave. I knew my daddy needed me there with him. In July I received a phone call from my husband and he had told me that I had been in Texas long enough. I told him daddy was getting a little stronger but not much. He told me to say my final goodbye because I will not be back. He was so mad at me.

But I didn't care. I felt that I had to put my father and my family first. I had all my children with me. I could not understand why he was so angry. It wasn't like he had to care for the kids by himself or anything. I ended up making my reservations to go back home. The day of my departure Daddy was lying on the sofa at Lisa's house. That morning I tried to wake him but he didn't budge. I kissed him goodbye. I then told my father I loved him. I looked at daddy and I seen his eye lashes move. I knew he was awake. I think he just didn't want to say goodbye to me. I know goodbyes were always hard for all of us. I flew back to California. David and Daniel kept the little ones busy the trip back. I think they knew that me leaving my father was very hard for me. I was so thankful because I had felt so lost after leaving Texas and my father. I was so afraid of losing him and me not being there with my family. I tried my best to think positive but it was so hard not to be afraid. I arrived back home in California but it was so hard not worrying about daddy. I called home as often as possible just to check on my father. I was still pretty hurt by my husbands comment to me while I was in Texas. I tried my best to stay busy and to think positive.

12

Then, on December 16th, I received a phone call around 8:00 p.m. The phone call was from my Brother Michael's son, Christopher. Christopher told me to call his daddy at the hospital and he started giving me the number. I asked him if Grandpa was all right, and he said "I don't know, Aunt Ruthie. Daddy just said for me to call you and to tell you to call him."

I told my nephew all right and I hung up the phone. I was so afraid to call, I started shaking. Then when I started to dial the number, I couldn't help myself from being terrified. The phone rang only once and Michael answered. Michael sounded so upset, it almost didn't sound like him. I asked him, "What, Michael, what? Is Daddy all right?"

Michael paused; gosh, it seemed like forever before he answered me. Then he said, "No Ruthie, everything is not all right. He's gone, Daddy died. We lost him, Ruthie, we lost our daddy."

Before I knew it, I had fainted. I felt so numb, I felt so empty. When I came to, I was so upset I just wanted to hug and be hugged by my brothers and sisters. I was hurting for myself and all of them.

Then I thought to myself, *oh my God, my daddy's gone. What are we going to do without him?* We had never been without Daddy before and Daddy was always there when we needed him. I knew that there was no way Daddy would ever leave us like Mom did.

Then I started thinking of my father's family. I thought to myself, *they must be devastated. I need to get to Texas. I need to be with all my family!* My husband at the time told me that we were going to drive back to Texas. My sister Lisa called back to see how I was doing. She was so distraught; she kept telling me that she didn't know what to do without our father. Lisa told me Michael was at her home making dinner for all of them and for Daddy. Lisa also said Daddy was lying on the couch when he died. I felt so bad for my sister that I just wanted to hug her and let her know we would all be together very soon. I told Lisa she didn't have to go through any of this alone. We would go through all of this together, just like we went through everything else during our lifetime together.

My sisters wanted me to fly home as soon as possible. They even told me to just go to the airport; they would have my tickets ready for me. They knew I had spent a lot of money going to be with Daddy so many times that same year. I told my husband that my sisters wanted me to fly home as soon as possible, but my husband would not hear of it. He told me, "We are driving and that is that." I was so mad at him for forcing me to drive back home. But I knew that I could not fly on my own I was to distraught to do anything on my own. It seemed like it took forever for me to get home.

The whole way, I didn't speak to my husband. I knew I was angry with him for not letting me go ahead of them to be with my family. I didn't even speak to my kids. I just remember crying and crying. I felt so bad because they adored their grandpa. But I was still angry at him for not letting me fly, and so torn up over my dad's death. I kept hearing my father's voice telling me he loved me, every Sunday when I called him. I kept thinking of seeing dad's eyelashes move the day I was leaving from Texas. I knew now if my father woke up that would have been his last goodbye to me. Now I know he just didn't want to say goodbye. Maybe daddy knew that would be the last time that he would see me. Gosh how am I going to say goodbye?

I know my kids were hurting as much as I was. But I was just too distraught to help them or to even try to console them. When we arrived in Galveston, we were to go to my Brother Willie's house. I found the key to his house under his mat, just like my sister-in-law had told me it would be. I hurried and showered and changed clothes as fast as I could. My boys were changing in the other bathroom. I had three small children at the time of my daddy's death and my husband was getting them ready.

The service was in a half an hour and I needed to be there. It was raining that night, and when we arrived, the boys and I jumped out of the van to avoid missing any of the service. My husband went to park the van with my other children. As I walked into the funeral home with my two boys, I saw my uncle Hoss. I hugged him and asked him where to go. Then he directed me through the doorway on the right. As I went into the funeral home, I saw so many people. The funeral home was completely full; every seat was taken. I saw so many good, close friends of my parents.

Then I saw my mother and my grandmother Ruth sitting with my sisters in the family room. I saw my little sister Patricia sitting in the family room as well. I guess she flew to the funeral with my mom. They were all in the family room together. But I didn't see any of my father's sisters or brothers in there. I still was not talking to my mother, so I walked out of the family room. I then walked towards my uncle Hoss. When I approached my uncle, I asked him where my aunts and uncles were. He told me they were sitting in the back of the funeral home on the last couple of pews.

I said, "Okay, I will go and find them" and I started walking. As I walked into the other part of the funeral home, I saw my two aunts and all my uncles sitting in the last couple of pews. I went up to my aunt Olivia and my aunt Janie and said, "Why are you way in the back?"

They both looked at me and said, "We wanted your sisters to be with your mom in the family room." They told me my sisters needed their mom right now. I just looked at them. But at the same time I saw so much pain in their faces. They were dying inside for their brother they just lost.

I told them their place was up front with my daddy. I told them Daddy would want them near him and that they were his sisters. I told them I needed them with me right by my father. They both stood up and hugged me and said, "Okay, let's go sit by your Daddy." I also told them I didn't want to be near my mom. They were okay with that. They knew everything that had happened between me and Mom. So they never really tried to convince me that I should forgive her or to try to talk to her. I really loved them for that. They just let me do what I felt was right for me and my family.

I just could not find a place in my heart to forgive Mom for all the pain she caused all of us. Even if my sisters needed Mom at that moment, that was okay with me. I didn't hold anything against them for that. They were very loving, just like Daddy. But I didn't need or want anything from mom. Before I knew it, we were walking towards Daddy. My aunts and my uncle Max walked to the first pew and my uncle Max and my two aunts sat right next to me.

As I looked up, I saw this beautiful coffin, and in it I could see my father's dark black hair. The coffin was so beautiful and classy, just like our father. There were many beautiful flowers everywhere. I was afraid to go up there and kneel by daddy. Three of my brothers were standing on one side and two were standing on the other. It was almost like they were guarding their father. They looked at me and I couldn't even get the strength to walk up to my own brothers.

Willie came up to me and hugged me, and then my sister-in-law came and hugged me. Willie told me he loved me. I looked at him and said, "I love you too, brother." Before I knew it, I had seen all my brothers and sisters. Each one of my brothers and sisters came up to me. We hugged like we never hugged before. I had never seen so much pain in all my life. Sandra left the family room and she came to sit with me and our aunts and uncles. I saw all of the people who mean the world to me in so much pain that day.

I was hurting so much inside, I almost didn't feel human; I felt like I was a machine just sitting there waiting. I never thought that we would ever lose our father. Daddy was like a mountain that would always stand there. Mom leaving us twice to go with Daddy's cousin was nothing compared to the pain our hearts were feeling right now.

My aunt Olivia looked at me and said, "Honey, let's go see your father, let him know you are here."

I looked at her and said, "I am so scared to see him, Aunt Olivia."

She then said, "Come on, I will go with you. Me and your Aunt Janie will go with you."

My aunt Olivia and my aunt Janie helped me to my feet. As we started walking towards the coffin, I started feeling my legs shaking. I think they felt it too, because they held on to me tighter. As we approached the coffin, I saw this great man lying there. I started thinking of when we were little and Daddy came back from one of his trips. I remember all the excitement in all of our faces when he walked in the room to let us know he was back from his trip.

Gosh, before I knew it, I had opened my eyes. There he was—my father. As we kneeled down in front of Daddy, I couldn't stop myself from crying. Daddy looked so handsome and peaceful. But then I was feeling so selfish inside. I wanted my father back and I didn't want God to take him from all of us. I started praying for my father and I told him we would all be together again very soon. I then leaned into the casket to kiss my father. My aunts then stood me up and turned me toward the pews. Before I knew it, hundreds of people were in line to give all of us their condolences. That was so hard hearing from all of these people how sorry they were for all of us. I knew everyone knew that we just lost a very great man. I started sobbing so much; I think it upset my husband.

When we went back to the pew to sit down, he walked up to me and said, "You need to help me with our kids and you need to stop crying, you are scaring them." I just looked at him. I didn't even respond. I thought to myself, *I hate him for not being sensitive to my feelings.* Daddy was a man who would have and did do anything for his kids. This was a man who was both parents to all of his kids for over 20 years. So I really didn't care what my husband thought.

The service was torture. There must have been hundreds of people there to pay their respects to my father. It seemed like everyone from Galveston Island was there. Everyone was giving condolences to my sisters in the family room and then to me and my father's family on the first two pews. It was so hard seeing all my family hurt so

95

much. I really feel that Daddy was a special brother because of all the pain he endured. I think that his family respected him so much for raising all his kids by himself.

Meanwhile, my mom was still in the family room. I couldn't understand why she thought that sitting in there was okay for her. She just has her morals all messed up. I know I would have been embarrassed to sit in the family room during the service of the man I abandoned and left with his cousin. I thought to myself, *as long as I can't see her, I will be okay.*

At the end of the service, everyone was starting to leave. Then, just as I looked up, I saw my mom, my grandmother Ruth, and my youngest sister, Patricia. They started walking towards my father's coffin. I froze and just as my mom and sister kneeled in front of Daddy's casket, my grandmother Ruth stood there and just looked at me. Before I knew it, I just started yelling at my mom to get away from Daddy and I told my grandmother the same thing.

My uncle Max grabbed me and told me to go outside with him. I was so upset, but I did as he asked. I felt like Mom had no right to be near this great man. The same man she hurt by marring his own cousin and having a baby with him. My uncle sat me in his car and drove me to my brother's house. I didn't even know where my kids were. I didn't even know where my husband was, and I really didn't care.

When we got to my brother's house, my uncle Max and I went into the bedroom. I couldn't stop myself from crying. I told my uncle I was very sorry; I didn't want to mess up Daddy's funeral. But I didn't think my mom had a right to be that close to him. My uncle hugged me and said, "Ruthie, your daddy and God want you to forgive your mom. Your father forgave her and so should you." He then said, "God doesn't want us to hate. And I don't want you with hate in your heart. I love you too much for that."

I just cried and said, "Uncle Max, I hate her for everything she did to all of us and to Daddy. I just don't want her anywhere near him." My uncle was such a good man; he had never talked bad about Mom to me or to my brothers and sisters before. Even now he didn't say anything negative about mom to me.

He just kept saying, "I know, I know." He just held me until I fell asleep. It felt so good knowing my uncle was there with me, especially since Daddy died.

I thought, *Oh God why can't I forgive Mom?* Then I started thinking, *why do I hate her so much?* I really didn't know why I was the one to feel so ugly towards Mom. All I knew was that I just couldn't forgive her!

I fell asleep, but before I knew it, I woke up. I looked at the clock and it was 3:00 a.m. I looked around me and my two girls were asleep on the other twin bed in the room I was in. As I got up, I walked into my nephew's bedroom and I saw my three boys asleep with my Brother Willie's stepsons. I went back into the room and just cried and prayed for God to give me strength to go through with my father's burial, which was in a few hours.

Before I knew it, we were on our way to the funeral home, then from there to the burial site. As I walked in the funeral home, I realized this would be the last time I would actually see my father. I already started feeling sick, and again I started shaking. I then realized I had not eaten anything. But I didn't care; I just wanted to spend as much time as I could with Daddy. I looked around the room and my sisters were all there crying and breaking apart inside and outside, just like me.

The priest and my cousin who was a pastor said a prayer before they were going to close the casket. As I watched in horror them closing the casket, I ran up to Daddy to kiss him one last time. I kissed him and I wanted so much for him to hug me and tell me he was in a better place now. I remember as they closed the casket, I started praying and talking to Daddy. I then said, "Daddy, thank you for being such a great father to all of us. You were the best father any girl would love to have. I love you, Daddy. I will always love you. I will always keep your memory alive. All of your grandchildren will know how great of a man you were. I promise, Daddy, I will never let anyone forget you!"

I started to cry. As I watched them close the casket, I knew that would be the last time I would see my loving father. I couldn't stop myself from crying and trembling. I felt so empty as I started walking towards the exit where my uncles were helping my sisters and me to the family car. I couldn't even touch my sisters to hug them. I think they felt as numb as I did. As I walked up to the family car, my aunt Janie came to me and said, "Ruthie, I will be here for you, okay?"

I looked at her and said "Okay." I saw as much sadness in my aunt as I did in my sisters and brothers. I felt so much closer to Daddy now that his sister was by my side. My aunt and my uncle helped me into the car and then my aunt went around to the other side to get in with me. Then, as I sat down, I noticed my mom was in the car too.

I looked up, and just as I reached for the door handle, my mom grabbed my hand and told me, "You better straighten up right now!" I snatched my hand away from hers and just as I did, my aunt opened the door. My aunt Janie saw my mom in the family car and she just grabbed me and pulled me out of the car without saying a word.

We stumbled to our feet and headed towards my father's oldest brother's car. My uncle Jesse seemed like he knew what had just happened, because he didn't even question why I was not with all my siblings. The ride to the burial site was horrific. It seemed like it took forever for us to get there. My mind was racing from one thing to another.

I was thinking of all the days we went to the beach as a family. I thought about those huge watermelons that were always so sweet. Then I started thinking of that big box that came in the mail so many years ago. I was thinking of how hard that must have been for Daddy to burn all of our things from Mom. I started remembering how happy Dad was when he went camping with all of our boys and his brother Max. I looked up, and my uncle Jesse was so quiet while he was driving and my aunt Rafe was sitting up front with him. I could see my Aunt Rafe crying. Then I looked to the side of me, and my aunt Janie was looking out the window, crying. I knew this was very hard for them, getting ready to bury their brother.

Then I thought, *they are not even thinking of their own pain. They are just thinking of being there for all their nieces and nephews. They were helping all the children of their brother. They are still helping their brother just like before. My family is so supportive of each other; I know my father is so very grateful to all of them for helping his children through this very difficult time in our lives.*

I prayed, "God, thank you for giving me such a great family." As we arrived at the cemetery, everyone was walking towards the area where they would lay my father to rest. Everyone started getting out of the car. Gosh, I just could not get my legs to move. As I tried to stand on my own two feet, I saw my brother Hector and his wife Jodie walking towards me. Just as Hector took my hand I felt numb.

I looked at my loving brother and said to him, "I don't want to say goodbye to Daddy, Hector I just can't say goodbye to him."

Hector just looked at me and smiled and said to me, "Everything will be all right, Sis. Daddy is resting now. He's not in any more pain."

Hector was crying and I looked at him and said, "I didn't even get to tell him I love him."

My sister-in-law Jodie looked at me and said, "Ruthie, your Daddy knows you loved him. He has always known all of you love him. Your daddy knew that every day of his life!"

Jodie and I were very good friends before she married my brother. When I looked at Jodie, she was hurting and so torn up, just like me and Hector. Jodie was very close with my father. She was the only girl who went camping with Daddy, Hector, and Uncle Max, and all of our boys. Jodie then started to cry, and she and Hector together helped me walk towards the burial site.

I saw all my sisters sitting under a canopy. As Hector sat me down, I looked up and again I saw my mom with my two older sisters. All of my brothers were standing together right by the casket, just like before. The priest gave Lisa Daddy's flag from being a veteran. Everything was so nice and proper for the type of man he was.

After the prayers were said in regards to my father, all of the daughters stood up to put a single rose on Daddy's casket. As I walked up to the casket, Lisa was standing there, already waiting for me. Lisa then took my hand and said, "Ruthie, Daddy told me that he wanted you to forgive Mom, so will you please try to do that for him?" She then took my hand and my mom's hand and placed them together. At that time, I just looked at my sister—the same person who raised me and showed me so much love throughout my life. I didn't want to hurt her or disrespect her. I pulled my hand gently away from my mother's. Then I looked at Lisa and said, "I can't, Lisa. I just can't." Then I just turned around and walked back to my seat.

I felt so empty without my father. I was afraid that my sister—the same person I adored—would be upset with me for not doing what she requested of me. Then I saw my sister and my mother sit down and I couldn't think of my mom again. I just wanted not to see my mother. My grandmother was still lurking around and I was so distraught, I didn't have the strength to go tell her off again. I just wanted the day to end.

13

I don't remember the drive back to Willie's house. I don't even remember how I got there. I just remember crying and thinking of so many different things that I shared with my brothers, my sisters, and our father. I remember walking through the front door of Willie's house and seeing my grandmother Ruth and Mom and my sister Patricia all sitting together on the sofa. I thought to myself, *these people just don't have any shame.* I then walked to the back bedroom that my sister-in-law had given me, and changed clothes. Afterwards, I just lay down on the bed to try to make myself go to sleep, pray for this day to hurry and end. When I woke up I noticed everyone had left except for Willie and his family. Willie told me that my uncles wanted to read my father's will before I went back to California. We made arrangements to meet that night. The reading of the will was very moving. Everyone remembered funny things that they experienced with daddy. I remember Michael started talking about when daddy took him and Ralph to get their hair cut. Michael said the barber was a little drunk and he nipped his ear. Michael said he yelled,"OUCH." Then Michael said my daddy walked over to him and licked his finger and rubbed Michael's ear to stop the bleeding. All of us started laughing and crying at the same time. All of us knew that was exactly how our father was with us.

The next day, I wanted to go by the cemetery before I left Texas. I went by, and it had rained so much the night before that everything was floating. All the flower arrangements and plants were floating around the area where my father was laid to rest. All of the flower arrangements were in a Christmas theme because Daddy died nine days before Christmas. By the time we buried our father, it was six days before Christmas. I looked around the burial site and thought, *God, why do these horrible things keep happening during the Christmas season? Our Mom leaving us twice and now our father dying so close to Christmas.*

I went back to California and I don't think I ever forgave my husband for being so mean and inconsiderate at my father's funeral. Christmas was very depressing and very hard for me. I tried my best to look happy for my kids, but I couldn't. I opened their presents with them and then just went into my room and cried for my father. Every Christmas holiday was like that for quite some time. During a three-week vacation, I started noticing my husband was very mean to my kids. I started talking with my kids and realized that my husband was a complete jerk to them the whole time during my marriage to him.

When I questioned my husband about it, he told me they needed to have discipline in their lives. We started arguing and arguing. I asked him if he ever even loved my kids. Or has he ever even told them that he loves them? I was stunned to hear his answer was "No." I knew at that moment I wanted out of this so called marriage. I should of known that someone that was so selfish at his wife's fathers funeral could not possibly love children that were not his. I filed for my divorce the very next day .I felt again that was a very good decision I made for myself and my three children who were not his. I knew that my father would never let anyone mistreat his grandchildren and I should not either. I then moved out of our home and into a four bedroom home of my own. I really started feeling happy again. One day I received a phone call from Willie. Willie asked me if I could do him a favor. I never said No to Willie before and I was not about to start now. I asked him what can I do. Willie started telling me that Mom left Arturo and moved back to Texas. He also said mom was going to file for a divorce. I asked Willie, what does this have to do with me? Willie started telling me that my mom needs to file for her divorce in California because Texas does not give spousal support to wives. Again I did not understand my Brother's request. Finally Willie asked me if I would allow my mom to come and live with me only until her divorce is final. I told Willie that I had not spoke to Mom in years. I also told him I didn't think I wanted her around my kids. Willie kept telling me that he really needed my help. So I ended up agreeing to his request. Willie told me mom will be flying to California soon. Willie said he would let me know when and where to pick mom up. On the day of my mother's arrival I went to the airport to pick her up with my children. I felt very uncomfortable when I seen her and I know she did too. My kids went up to her and hugged her and David grabbed her suitcase and started walking to the car. I didn't even say hi to my mom. I just could not get myself to forget everything that she did to all of us. Mom kept talking to the kids but I could tell she was very uncomfortable with me. As time went on I tried my best to treat my mom decent. I told myself I was going to try for myself and my kids. One day I was talking on the phone to my Aunt Olivia. When I finished with my phone call I walked out of my room and I heard my mom talking to my daughter Sondra. My mom was saying that she didn't understand why I treat my Aunts so great. Then my mom said,"I don't know why your mom wastes her money on calling them every Sunday." I started fuming. I rushed down the stairs and into the den where my mom and Sondra were standing. I then started to tell my mom not to talk bad about anyone in my dad's family to my children. My mom started telling me that my dad's family are no good and that I should not trust any of them. I started telling my mom that I will always trust my dad's family. I also said to her that it is her I can not trust. Then before I knew it my mom started saying really bad things about my Aunt Olivia. My mom told me that my Aunt Olivia thought that I was not the daughter of my father that I am from her husband, my Uncle Hoss. I froze as I heard this and I

A Father's Love

103

demanded that she leave my house right then and there. I ran upstairs and called my son David to come and pick up his grandmother and to take her to his home. After I made that phone call I called Willie and told him that I can no longer have my mother in my home. I started to tell Willie everything mom said to me. Willie told me not to worry that daddy is my father and that he doesn't know why my mom would say such a thing .He also said nothing can change that my whole life I was daddy's daughter. I tried my best to listen but I was hurt and confused. I heard David leave with my mom. I just laid down on my bed and cried. Before I knew it I had dialed my Aunt Olivia and my Uncle Hoss' house .My Aunt Olivia answered the phone and I started telling her everything that my mother said. My Aunt Olivia told me that my uncle loved my father very much and he would never do anything to hurt him. She also said that my uncle respected my father too much to do anything like that to him. After talking on the phone with my Aunt I decided to fly back home and ask my uncle myself. I arrived in Texas and I went straight to my Aunt and Uncle's house. I walked inside to talk to my Aunt and I had asked her where could I find my Uncle? My Aunt said he is waiting for you under the tree out side. As I started walking out side I saw my uncle sitting quietly under the tree. I went up to him and told him hello and kissed him on his cheek. He looked up at me and smiled and said,"hello movie star." I smiled back at him and said." Hi Uncle Hoss." Uncle Hoss always called me movie star I guess because I lived in California. I just looked at him at first I wasn't sure how I was going to bring it up. But before I knew it I did. I had already started telling him what my mother said. Before I could finish, my loving Uncle grabbed my hand and said," Ruthie I love all of you very much and I would be proud if you were my daughter, but there is no way that is possible. You see I have never been with your mother. I am not sure why she would say such a thing but I love and respect your daddy too much to ever do anything like that to him. I am sorry but I do love you Ruthie." I just started crying and we sat there and hugged each other. I never questioned my paternity again after that. I think my mother just wanted me to hate my father's family so she said that horrible lie to hurt me. I still question WHY? Why would a mother want to hurt her daughter that way? I feel I have been hurt enough with the childhood I was handed from my mother. I really feel it is time for me to stop hurting.

14

Years went by, and later I met the love of my life. His name is David; we call him D.J. We were married in March of 2003. My husband D.J. took me to Texas to get married in front of everyone who means the world to me. I was so grateful to him and I feel that my father was right there with me and his son-in-law, sharing our special day. I know my dad would have loved D.J. My dad would have been very grateful to D.J. for being so unselfish by taking me home to get married, instead of marrying me in California with his family. My father's brother gave me away at my wedding. My Uncle Max was there when mom left us. Then I remember him hugging us when our house caught on fire. But when we lost daddy my uncle Max never left my side. I know daddy thanks him for being such a great Uncle and a even greater Brother. I know I can't ever thank him enough for always being there for me and all of my brothers and sisters. He is truly the best I thank God for him every day...

I am truly happy now. The one and only thing I wish is that my father could see that I finally found true love and happiness. D.J. tells me all the time that he wishes he had met my father, but that he feels that he knows him through me and my family. So I know I kept my promise I made to my father at his funeral, to keep his memory alive. It has been 12 years since we lost Daddy, and even now 12 years later, every time anyone visits Daddy's grave, there's flowers or some type of arrangement on his tombstone.

I really feel everyone still misses him and mourns him. My younger children were two and three years old when my father died. But even now, they tell me they feel like they know him through me. Gosh, that is such a good feeling. Before my wedding, my youngest son Richard won a gold medal for wrestling in school. When D.J. and I went to visit my father's grave, we saw Richard had left his medal on the grave of his grandpa. That day I felt so proud of my son for thinking of his grandfather.

I feel all my children and all of my siblings' children love their grandfather very much, even though they did not know him as well as all the others. They tell me they love him so much for being such a great father to me. I sure hope they will spread his memory to their children on how great of a grandfather they had.

A few months after I was married, I lost my uncle Fedencio, my father's brother. After the funeral services, I called Texas to see how the services went, and how my uncle's wife was doing. My sister told me that my uncle said that he had seen my father, and that my father told him "not to forget the papers." I figured Daddy knew Uncle Fedencio was going to join him in heaven. But I could not understand what Daddy meant by saying "Don't forget the papers."

After speaking to my sister Lilly, I remembered some papers I had from my uncle that he had sent to me right after Daddy died. I started reading everything from the time of my father's death and even some things from before Daddy died. Then I started reading the paperwork from the funeral. I noticed a discrepancy with who paid what for my father's services. I tossed and turned all night trying to understand my findings.

The next morning I contacted the funeral home and asked them who paid for my father's services. The woman at the funeral home faxed me a copy of the agreement. I found out a different insurance company paid for my father's services, not my father's employment life insurance. Then I contacted my father's work to ask why they did not pay for my father's services 12 years ago. After researching, my father's union discovered that they never paid my family for my father's retirement pension. I was so stunned and appalled that I gave them 30 days to pay us the money they owed all of us. I told them that they should be ashamed of themselves, not paying the president of their union. I told them that Daddy died knowing he was leaving all of his 11 kids with something, and they didn't do what they were supposed to do.

I also told them that my father gave them 35 years of service. And that for 30 years, he was "THEIR PRESIDENT." I told them my father was so loyal to all of them even in death, that on his tombstone it reads "PREZ" which was my father's nickname on the waterfront.

I guess they knew I was angry with them, because finally on the 29th day, we received payment on the balance of my father's retirement pension. This payment was over 105,000 dollars. I contacted my brothers and sisters and told them that my husband D.J. and I were flying home with some shocking news. I had only shared my discovery with Michael and Sandra at the time. I wanted to make sure my findings were not a mistake before I told everyone.

I had contacted my uncle Jesse who was one of my father's beneficiaries at the time of his death. When I arrived in Texas, my uncle Jesse had a meeting at my father's home for all of us to go over my findings with everyone. My uncle gave me the check to divide among all 11 of us. We then divided the check among all of my father's children. We had decided to include my nephew Jesse, since Daddy had adopted him. Everyone agreed that was what Daddy would want.

Everyone was so excited to receive so many thousands of dollars. I think every one thought that it was too good to be true. I cried during each check I wrote. Even Patricia drove to Texas to get her check. Patricia lives in California still, but for some unknown reason, she stopped coming over to my home and even stopped talking to me. But I figured that I couldn't try with someone who didn't understand what happened to all of us so many years ago. After all, she was not raised by my father; she was raised by Arturo.

109

I decided I was going to just leave her alone and enjoy my family and all of my memories.

As I handed out the checks, everyone was pretty choked up when it was their turn. I recall that when I wrote the check for my sister Patricia, I told her that even though Daddy didn't raise her, he loved her, and even now, 12 years later, he was still taking care of her. I told her that Daddy loved her and I wished she would have known him like all of us did.

I am not sure if she really understands how lucky she is to have had a father like that. But someday maybe she will.

During the meeting, I had dedicated a song for Daddy after we passed out the checks to everyone. All of us sat and listened for four minutes to the song dedicated to him. Everyone was crying and feeling our father in that house, the same house we were all raised in—the same house that my mother abandoned us in.

I started to look around me and it was almost as if I could see my father walking past us and telling all of us that he will always be with us. I was sitting on the stairs in the living room being hugged by my husband, and I was feeling so torn up inside, missing my father.

I remembered when I was sitting there years ago with Michael, not knowing that we would be hurt again from Mom leaving us for the second time. I looked over at Michael and Ralphy and Sandra, and they looked as devastated as we all did at the funeral. I knew that day that Daddy will always be there if we ever needed to talk to him. I told my brothers and sisters that I will continue to search every avenue to make sure everything that is owed to our father is paid to all of us. I feel we owe that to our father, since he worked so hard for all of us his whole life. I also told all my brothers and sisters that even now, 12 years after Daddy's death, he was still taking care of each and every one of us!

Right now I am looking up at the sky, and I pray to my loving father, saying, "Thank you, Daddy, for being such a great father and thank you for never giving up on any of us." You were always there for all of us, and I thank you for that. When I was a little girl, I always knew that when I came home from school, you would still be there. I AM SO PROUD TO HAVE BEEN YOUR DAUGHTER AND I AM EVEN MORE PROUD THAT YOU ARE MY FATHER. I WILL NEVER FORGET YOU, DADDY, OR ALL OF THE SACRIFICES YOU MADE FOR ALL OF YOUR CHILDREN AND THE SACRIFICES YOU MADE FOR ME!!!!!!! I WILL FOREVER MISS ALL OF YOUR EMBRACES AND ALL OF THE LOVE YOU GAVE TO ME!!! I LOVE YOU, DADDY, AND YOU WILL ALWAYS BE WITH ME IN MY HEART!!!

There are two things I have learned from having such a great father: First I know there is nothing stronger than "A FATHER'S LOVE" and second, no matter what," EVEN A DOG DOESN"T LEAVE HER PUPPIES!!!!!!"

THE END

This is a special thank you to all of the Sendejas Family. Thank you so much for loving me and always being there for me and my brothers and sisters. I am so proud to call each and every one of you my family!!!

To the Hernandez Family
Thank you all for your understanding and your love during the writing of this book. My life is so complete with all of you as my Family I am very proud to say I AM A HERNANDEZ.

About the Author

Ruthie Hernandez is a loving wife, mother, and grandmother. She resides in southern California with her loving family. There is not a day that goes by when Ruthie does not thank God for giving her such a great and loving Father.

Printed in the United States
22696LVS00005B/160-168

9 781418 475161